ACTIVE LEARNING
in NINETY MINUTES

For a complete list of Management Books 2000 titles, visit our website on www.mb2000.com

---

The original idea for the 'In Ninety Minutes' series was presented to the publishers by Graham Willmott, author of 'Forget Debt in Ninety Minutes'. Thanks are due to him for suggesting what has become a major series to help business people, entrepreneurs, managers, supervisors and others to greatly improve their personal performance, after just a short period of study.

Proposed titles in the 'in Ninety Minutes' series are:

Forget Debt in Ninety Minutes
Understand Accounts in Ninety Minutes
Working Together in Ninety Minutes
Supply Chain in Ninety Minutes
Networking in Ninety Minutes
25 Management Techniques in Ninety Minutes
Practical Negotiating in Ninety Minutes
Find That Job in Ninety Minutes
Control Credit in Ninety Minutes
Faster Promotions in Ninety Minutes
Managing Your Boss in Ninety Minutes
Better Budgeting in Ninety Minutes
... other titles may be added

The series editor is James Alexander

Submissions of possible titles for this series or for management books in general will be welcome. MB2000 are always keen to discuss possible new works that might be added to their extensive list of books for people who mean business.

ACTIVE LEARNING in 90 Minutes

THE BOOK THAT IS ALSO

A SELF-MANAGED PERSONAL DEVELOPMENT PROGRAMME

Allan Scott

2000

First published in 2005 by Management Books 2000 Ltd
Forge House, Limes Road
Kemble, Cirencester
Gloucestershire, GL7 6AD, UK
Tel: 0044 (0) 1285 771441/2
Fax: 0044 (0) 1285 771055
E-mail: info@ mb2000.com
Web: www.mb2000.com

Printed and bound in Great Britain by Digital Books Logistics Ltd of Peterborough

British Library Cataloguing in Publication Data is available

ISBN 1-85252-477-4

339026

Contents

Overview   6

Introduction   9
    Using a mentor   10
    Modules   12
    Project criteria   14
    Role realignment   15
    Charts and illustrations   17

Module #1: People Management a: leading people   **19**
    Personal Progress Review: Module #1   41

Module #2: People management b: developing people   **47**
    Personal progress review: Module #2   74

Module #3: Project management   **77**
    Personal progress review: Module #3   101

Module #4: Self management   **104**
    Personal progress review: Module #4   148

Total review   **152**

Index   **155**

5

ACTIVE LEARNING - THE BOOK THAT IS ALSO A SELF-MANAGED PERSONAL DEVELOPMENT PROGRAMME

An overview of the Active Learning method

It is still the case in many organisations, industrial, commercial, financial, charitable, even educational, that managers are selected primarily for their knowledge of the main productive process in which the organisation is engaged. Whatever else may be required in the appointment, is too often given little consideration. As a result, people who have good technical knowledge and ability, which may have taken years of hard effort to acquire, can find themselves faced with a raft of new responsibilities which may quickly become the real determinants of success or failure in the appointment, but in which they have little or no knowledge or experience.

For those people in particular, but also for any manager who is not as well rounded in management skills as the job requires, this book provides access to the basic elements of good management techniques in four of the key areas of responsibility of any management appointment. It also provides a starting point for the acquisition of essential skills through the real time experience of **Active Learning**.

Active Learning involves the process of **learning-by-doing**, the same process we use when learning to ride a bicycle or drive a car. In this case, what you will be learning to do is to become a better manager by working though a series of four Active Learning modules. These describe good management and leadership practices, and provide techniques which you can put immediately into actual use within the operational requirements of your own appointment.

Using Active Learning to reinforce the guidance given, you will be helped to make to make adjustments that are appropriate to your individual needs and relevant to your individual responsibilities. **There is no work time lost on off-the-job training.**

The Active Learning programme gives you a comprehensive personal learning schedule for improving performance in four key results areas:

- **establishing yourself as the leader and getting people to work for you**

- **getting the best out of people and keeping them controlled and disciplined**

- **organising work projects and keeping activities progressing**

- **developing your ability to meet different demands of the appointment, and keeping yourself progressing.**

> ☞ If you are a first time manager, you will find it an ideal method of helping you to become competent in dealing with your new responsibilities.
>
> ☞ If you are already in management, but have little or no formal management training, you will find it an effective way of extending the knowledge and skills you have already acquired.

The process actively involves you in the **key aspects** of your appointment, encourages you to think proactively about the nature and scope of your responsibilities, and quickly produces beneficial results. Even if there are sections where you decide it is not practical or possible or necessary to follow the action recommended in the programme, the assessment you will have made in order to arrive at that decision will have actively helped to develop your management judgement.

At the end of the programme, you will have:

- obtained a better understanding of good management and leadership practices

- gained hands-on Active Learning experience of good practice techniques within the operational requirements of your own appointment

- made more productive use of working hours

- been helped to develop your management judgement

- gained in knowledge, confidence, and self-reliance

- a better ability to produce results at the standards of performance and levels of achievement required in the appointment

- a personal file of good practice techniques that can be referred to an any time in your future career.

Introduction

The Active Learning programme is designed to help you develop your potential for managing in a way that allows for your own individuality and which, by providing you with the guidance needed to extend your repertoire of skills, abilities and knowledge, enables you to learn by experience within the particular context of your present appointment.

☑ **Check Points within the guidance notes will enable you to identify exactly where you may need to revise your approach.**

☞ This is one of the important new books in the *'in Ninety Minutes'* series. Although we will be talking about taking several weeks to complete each learning module, it is strongly recommended that you take an hour and a half or so to read swiftly through this book to gain a clear and encouraging insight into the whole process. Then you will be better equipped to follow the suggestions for each section in turn.

Your programme consists of four self-managed **Active Learning modules**. How long you take to work through each module will depend on the circumstances of your appointment, but typically you are likely to find that each module 'runs' for four weeks, but may be extended to eight weeks depending on your progress. Each module provides guidance notes to assist your understanding of the principles involved, and describes best-practice techniques which you can adapt and put immediately into actual use to meet the requirements of your appointment.

The modules can be taken in any order and you will get the best results by working through only one module at a time.

At the end of each module, you will be asked to review the actions you have taken and record the progress made. This visual record will show how well your personal development is progressing from the level held at commencement of the programme.

- By reinforcing good management and leadership practices, development projects of this kind can quickly produce improved results. However, it is not advisable to try to accelerate the development of your knowledge and skills at a pace that makes it difficult for you or your subordinates to adjust to changes in methods and emphasis of approach.

- Since this is a self-managed project, you will need to judge what is an appropriate pace for proceeding, but that does not mean that you should continually defer from taking action or hold back from introducing change where it is appropriate to do so, nor does it mean you should try to make changes where none are required.

- It is also important to remember that no actions or changes that might affect or alter operational arrangements with other internal departments or with external customers, clients, or other agencies should be made without first securing appropriate agreement with those involved.

No actions or changes that might affect or alter company policy should be made without first obtaining appropriate senior authority.

Using a mentor

Although this programme is designed for you to work through on your own, you may find it helpful to discuss particular issues with a more experienced colleague from whom you can seek advice, and who may agree to assist you with a **mentoring arrangement**.

A mentoring arrangement is more than just a casual undertaking in which you occasionally ask for and receive advice. It is about a relationship in which the more experienced employee (the mentor) provides support and encouragement, as well as advice and guidance, to help you develop the knowledge and skills required in your appointment.

The mentor will need to make himself familiar with the purpose, content, and objectives of your programme, but you should not expect him to take any active part in working through the modules. His role is to advise and encourage, and to provide access to an experienced knowledge of organisational and procedural matters that would be impossible for you to accumulate in the time you have set yourself to complete the programme.

It is usual for the mentor to be your immediate senior, but in particular cases the mentor may be a training or human resource specialist. Whichever the case, the mentor must have sufficient knowledge and experience of the activities involved to be able to give the support required.

In agreeing to act as your mentor, your colleague will be signalling his support for your personal effort to improve your situation, and will try to encourage you to maintain the momentum of commitment and effort the programme requires. That support may substantially increase the progress you are able to make, but it will be up to you to learn from the experience, to develop the knowledge and skills described, and to carry the programme through to a successful conclusion.

For a range of excellent books on the process of mentoring, visit the **mb2000.com** website, and look for books by Mike Pegg.

Active Learning

Modules

Module #1: People management (a) leading people

Leadership

Team-building; developing self-esteem; communicating;
gaining commitment

Motivating; building morale

Internal relationships; well-being; conflict management

Personal progress review: Module #1

Module #2: People management (b) developing people

Skills assessment and training; development support review

Performance standards and goal setting

Empowerment; Delegation

Disciplines; Controls

Personal progress review: Module #2

Module #3: Project management

Planning a project; constructing an operational plan;
preparing a project calendar; developing planning skill

Managing a project; setting up controls and monitor systems;
updating information; dealing with problems

Concluding a project; calculating end results; evaluating
performance; analysing what went right and wrong;

producing and distributing an end of project report; reviewing overall effectiveness

Problem solving; generating solutions

Personal progress review: Module#3

Module #4: Self management

Managing your time

Making your decisions

Improving your communication

Handling change; putting change into effect; overcoming resistance to change

Handling pressure: dealing with temporary pressures and accumulations

PR: Promoting the business image

Required personal enhancement

Personal progress review: Module #4

Total review

Total review of your personal development progress; continuing your personal development programme

On completion, the module guidance notes will provide you with unique personal points of reference on management and leadership activities that you can consult at any time in your future career.

Project criteria

Given the wide variation in operating procedures that exist in business, you may find it necessary for particular techniques to be adapted to meet the circumstances of your appointment, but any changes should be consistent with the principles described in the programme, and with achieving the objectives set out below.

Building leadership skills

Taking positive action to lead rather than dictate, setting examples, communicating, gaining commitment, developing team spirit and team effort. Reinforcing motivation and morale, fostering good internal relationships, showing concern for employees' well-being, effectively resolving interpersonal conflict.

Developing people

Obtaining adequate knowledge of peoples' abilities and training needs, providing appropriate training and development opportunities, actively supporting development of knowledge and skills through empowerment and delegation, setting appropriate performance standards and goals, applying appropriate disciplines and controls.

Planning and organising

Thinking ahead, anticipating and predicting potential outcomes, establishing and maintaining an appropriate course of action to accomplish a goal, including setting objectives, aligning priorities, assessing resources, setting up appropriate controls and monitor systems.

Problem solving

Understanding the type of problem to be dealt with, taking appropriate steps to determine its nature and cause, using appropriate methods to generate and find a solution, and taking action to rectify the situation.

Self-management

Being personally well organised, making effective use of time, keeping focused on key results areas, taking initiatives, actively influencing events rather than passively accepting, seeing opportunities, acting on them, and getting things done.

Being decisive

Showing a readiness to make decisions, state opinions, and take action. Exercising judgement, showing an ability to evaluate data and courses of action, interpret information, test opinions, identify consequences. and reach logical conclusions. Making an unbiased and rational assessment, recognising flaws or gaps, and discriminating between factual and unsubstantiated evidence.

Communicating well

Being able to get information, instructions, knowledge, and ideas across in the most effective way. Being able to develop well written reports, and well constructed written and verbal presentations.

Handling change

Identifying the source, nature and purpose of change, calculating necessary adjustments, anticipating potential problems, preparing practical steps for implementation, putting the change into effect, and using appropriate methods to overcome any employee resistance.

Handling pressure

Identifying the causes and effects of pressure, taking appropriate action to deal with exceptional one-off situations, understanding and taking appropriate action to deal with an accumulation of different pressures.

PR: External relationships

Taking action to promote the company's image and reputation in line with its public relations objectives, including maintaining business communication at a high level of professionalism, developing good customer relations, keeping to specific arrangements, and encouraging staff members to promote a positive image of professionalism in their contacts and dealings with others.

Being forward looking
Taking steps to maintain a successful, ongoing, programme of personal development.

Role re-alignment

This development programme supports a role re-alignment from Manager to Leader. As you work through the Modules, you may find some of the activities require you to adopt a new approach to some of the responsibilities of your appointment. The following is a list of the areas where some adjustment may be necessary, and for which guidance is provided.

Manager role	- re-aligning to leader role
Being a boss	- re-aligning to being a coach and facilitator
Controlling people	- re-aligning to empowering people
Being aggressive	- re-aligning to being assertive
Centralising authority	- re-aligning to distributing authority
Directing with rules and regulations	- re-aligning to guiding with shared values and an open culture
Establishing status power and hierarchy	- re-aligning to building relationship power and team values
Demanding compliance	- re-aligning to gaining commitment
Focusing on numbers tasks	- re-aligning to focusing on quality, and customers and service
Confronting and combating	- re-aligning to collaborating and unifying

Stressing independence - re-aligning to fostering independence

Being internally competitive - re-aligning to being internally supportive and externally competitive

Changing by necessity - re-aligning to continuously learning,
and crisis   improving and innovating

Charts and illustrations

Grid 1: review of key team activities

Grid 2: team members' ability values

Self-rated assessment form

Checklist of readiness for empowerment

Daily task sheet

Project calendar example

Checklist of personal enhancement

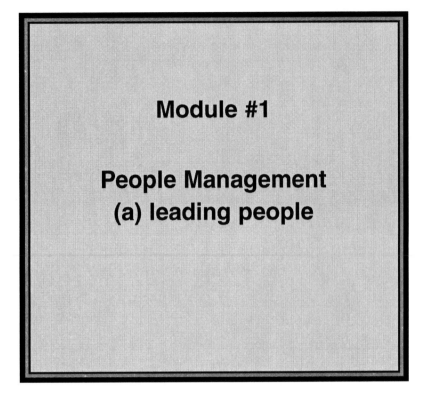

Module #1

People Management
(a) leading people

Start date for this module _____

Leadership

'I'm just a hired jack - a professional manager. I'm proud of that. I'm not a proprietor, not dominant. I lead by example and persuasion and a hell of a lot of hard work. Not on the basis of power and authority. My skills are to help people release their energies and focus themselves, and helping them achieve a common aim. People only do things they are convinced about. One has to create the conditions in which people want to give of their best.'

Sir John Harvey-Jones

It is no coincidence that **Leadership** is the first of the key results areas of management responsibility covered in this programme. It is not only the natural starting point for developing management ability, but is also a prerequisite for effectiveness in all other areas of management activity. How you act as a leader will underwrite your authority and your performance as a team builder, an organiser, a planner, a decision maker, a problem solver, an achiever of objectives, and in any other aspect of management in which you become involved.

The relation between **leading** and **managing** is an overlapping one. It is certain that every effective leader must firstly be a manager, but it does not follow that every manager is an effective leader. While the manager's primary responsibility is for getting things done by effective use of the resources available, the leader will embrace this responsibility, but will do more. He will additionally apply a high level of commitment to understanding the needs, concerns, and aspirations of the people who work for him. He will genuinely help and encourage them to make the best use of their abilities and to develop their knowledge and skills to the mutual benefit of themselves and the organisation in which they are employed.

It is a fundamental of business that while the manager must retain overall accountability for performance, practical responsibility for activities operates best at the level at which the activities are conducted. Allocating practical responsibility for local day-to-day activities to the employees concerned, increases their involvement. It creates conditions likely to improve commitment and the development of their knowledge and skills, and makes it easier for the manager to achieve an overview of events and retain overall control.

However, people are naturally individuals, they have different talents, and motivations, and some will be more hard-working and conscientious than others. Just because five or six people are working within the same department, it does not automatically mean that if left to themselves they will work co-operatively towards a common goal. Individual performance may be good, but unless they are working co-operatively towards a common goal, the overall result may be less than required.

The key to co-operative achievement is good leadership. It should be assertive, firm, sure; a positive statement of the leader's personal values applied with purpose, assurance and conviction, but not dominating or aggressive. It should be reflected in the standards the leader sets for himself and others; standards of commitment, performance, behaviour, support, and loyalty. Well defined, it will encourage a confident performance from team members who will feel they know what is expected of them, and where they stand in the relationships. Ill defined, it will lead to uncertainties and failures.

In those terms, good leadership can be considered as much a part of the assets a manager brings to his job as his technical knowledge, or his commercial awareness, and as much a part of his skills in utilising resources as his ability to plan, organise, or schedule activities.

For those reasons, the following guidance notes describe good practice techniques that will help you develop a style of leading that will enable you to get people working co-operatively towards a common goal, and will help you to more effectively meet the specific requirements of this key area of your management responsibilities.

Team building

It is generally accepted that the most effective way to increase the overall performance capability of a group of employees is for the manager to adopt the role of leader, and begin to create an active working team.

While retaining overall responsibility for the management and control of equipment, materials, and peoples' activities, a leader will additionally take steps to develop a working unity of purpose by encouraging **commitment to a common goal.** He will harness the individual talents, motivations, and ambitions of group members to obtain a level of performance that is greater than the total individual contributions.

As leader, you will need to establish the team's purpose and identity.

The team will need to know why it is being formed and what it is trying to achieve. You will need to explain what is to be achieved, which members of the working group will be needed to accomplish that purpose, and how by working more closely to combine and share their collective skills and knowledge as an active team they can increase their overall performance capability.

☑ I already do this [ ]   I need to revise my approach [ ]

You may find it helpful to developing what you want to convey to the team about its purpose and identity if you draft out a **Statement of Team Purpose and Identity** in the box below. (In some organisations this is referred to as a *Mission Statement.*)

21

DRAFT STATEMENT OF TEAM PURPOSE AND IDENTITY

As leader, you will need to create a team spirit.

Most working groups do not develop into effective teams without deliberate team building activities on the part of the leader. There are several steps commonly used in team building.

- **Define the nature and characteristics of team membership** by involving all members in constructive discussion about team goals and objectives, assigned roles, and the need for openness, trust, loyalty and support. Discuss processes for solving problems or disputes, and establish any necessary new rules and procedures. All members should be encouraged to contribute to these discussions, but decisions should be guided by the leader.

22

I already do this [ ]   I need to revise my approach [ ]

● **Sort out the growing pains** by understanding that members will react in different ways to the nature of team activity and the demands placed on them. Some will find it easier than others to work closely with team colleagues, and some may try to extend their influence over others. Some may find it difficult to share their knowledge or skills.

Differences will emerge in terms of individual and group commitment, task priority, and styles and methods of working. There may be misunderstandings about who does what or who has the right to do this or that. There may be disagreement about how best to schedule particular activities. It will be necessary for these differences, misunderstandings, and disagreements to come out into the open, and for the leader to exert a controlling influence to resolve them harmoniously to prevent future undermining of team efforts.

 I already do this [ ]   I need to revise my approach [ ]

● **Create cohesion** by encouraging members to begin by undertaking relatively undemanding tasks that need them to think less of their differences and more about how their individual roles and responsibilities can relate and combine to achieve their objectives. This will help them develop co-operative working practices, to gain better respect for each other's abilities, and to begin forming a relationship of trust and confidence that will enable them to undertake more demanding assignments.

 I already do this [ ]   I need to revise my approach [ ]

● **Keep things developing and moving** by acknowledging achievements and raising expectations to strengthen the members' commitment to team working and team objectives. At this stage the team should begin to generate its own energy and

23

should be kept developing and moving forward. It may be necessary to consider further training for individuals, or there may be opportunities for role and task flexibility to extend skills and knowledge, or it may be possible to look for ways to extend or broaden the team's activities.

☑ I already do this [ ]   I need to revise my approach [ ]

As leader, you will need to know the extent of individual people's capabilities, will need to make a point of noting their strengths and weaknesses, and will need to provide conditions that will enable them to make best use of their skills, and their best contribution to team effort.

Even in groups of people performing similar routine tasks, some will be better at particular aspects than others. Knowing this will enable you to see where it is necessary and possible for team members to help each other. By encouraging closer co-operation of this kind you will get best use of their skills and knowledge. You will also obtain their best contribution to team effort, and develop a sense of team unity and loyalty that will begin to hold the group together voluntarily.

☑ I already do this [ ]   I need to revise my approach [ ]

Use the grids set out on the following two pages to make an initial evaluation of the team's strengths and weaknesses. Use them again if the team's purpose or identity changes.

Review of key team activities

Decide which are the key activities of the team and write them into the grid below in descending order of importance. These are the activities on which team performance will be judged, and around which you will need to assess and then develop the contribution of individual members.

N.B. This grid makes provision for six key activities. This will be sufficient for most teams, but if you consider your team has more than six key activities, decide which are the six most important and use only those.

Key activity	Brief description
#1	
#2	
#3	
#4	
#5	
#6	

Evaluation of team members' abilities

For each of the six key team activities, use the following scale of values in which 3 is the benchmark level of ability required, to record your realistic evaluation of each member's ability to carry out the activity involved. List all team members, but since not all of the team will necessarily be involved in all of the activities, only record value scale entries against those activities in which a member is involved. Use initials to identify team members.

Value 1: Does not have enough knowledge or skill to carry out the activity. Urgently requires training or assistance.
Value 2: Knows what needs to be done, but finds it difficult. Would benefit from further training or assistance.
Value 3: Has adequate knowledge and skill to carry out the activity. Does not need further training or assistance at present.
Value 4: Has good knowledge and skill in the activity. Could train or assist others.

Member	Key activity 1				Key activity 2				Key activity 3				Key activity 4				Key activity 5				Key activity 6			
	1	2	3	4	1	2	3	4	1	2	3	4	1	2	3	4	1	2	3	4	1	2	3	4

Developing self-esteem

As leader, you will need to develop the self-esteem of team members

People perform best if they feel their abilities and contributions are recognised and appreciated. You should be prepared to show that while your first concern is for the collective performance of your team, you value members for their unique abilities, and recognise their contributions to team results. You should be prepared to show your appreciation of individual effort, and should take every opportunity to give positive feedback about the team to other parts of the business.

 I already do this [ ]   I need to revise my approach [ ]

Communicating

As leader, you will need to keep members informed and up to date, will need to relay relevant information on a timely basis, and will need to encourage debate and discussion about team matters

Team members will not only need to know of any matters that directly relate to their individual activities, but in order to retain their involvement in and commitment to the team's performance, should be kept aware of any information of general relevance or usefulness to team activities. Remember, the best communication process is a two-way one. Members should be permitted to speak candidly about team issues, without fear of recrimination, and should be encouraged to put forward ideas and suggestions that might assist or improve team effort. They should be listened to with genuine interest.

 I already do this [ ]   I need to revise my approach [ ]

Gaining commitment

As leader, you will need to gain commitment to team objectives, and an acceptance of individual roles and responsibilities as part of a team performance.

It is not always easy for people to adjust from working as individuals. You will need to show a personal commitment to team working and team objectives to encourage other members to do the same. You will need to define clear roles for each person, including yourself, and will need to ensure that each member can understand and accept the areas of responsibility he or she is accountable for, and how they relate to the responsibilities of other members and the overall objectives of the team.

 I already do this [ ] I need to revise my approach [ ]

As leader you will need to identify with and approve the team's task requirements with real commitment before asking the commitment of others.

The question of moral or ethical considerations may not arise very often in most business situations, but even in day to day matters, team members will trust you to question, understand and approve the intention and content of an activity before asking for their commitment to it. They will hold back if they feel you are asking them to do something, but have not bought into it yourself.

 I already do this [ ] I need to revise my approach [ ]

As leader, you will need to remain involved and approachable, will need to listen with genuine interest, and will need to take positive action to respond to any matters raised

It is not enough to simply adopt an 'open door' attitude and wait for members to make an approach. Without acting officiously, you will achieve a better knowledge of how things are progressing, and will be better able to identify potential problems, if you show a genuine interest in each member's activities. It doesn't pay to ignore signs that a team member is unhappy or is being 'bugged' by something. Ask about it. By listening with interest to any situations or problems members need help with, and by taking prompt and positive action to assist, you will confirm your own commitment to the team.

 I already do this [ ]   I need to revise my approach [ ]

Motivation and Building Morale

Motivation and morale are closely related behavioural states which not only interact with each other, but can be directly influenced by a wide range of conditions. These include the relationships between people and, particularly in team situations, by the relationship between the leader and team members.

Motives and morale are individualistic. Because they are based on needs and values, they vary from person to person. An incentive or a success for one person may represent a deterrent or a failure for another. They are also subject to change. What motivates a person today, may not have that effect tomorrow; what gives a feeling of confidence and well-being may be quickly replaced by something that creates doubt and uncertainty.

However, although motivation and morale are internally personalised conditions, it is certain that people do not work just for obscure personal urges. In any work situation, however conscientious and committed people may be, and however hard they may work to meet the needs of their appointment, they will want to gain something tangible for themselves out of what they do. By taking time to discuss and find out what employees find easy or hard, or rewarding or displeasing about the tasks they perform, and what it is they want to gain for themselves, it is possible for the leader to find how best to improve motivation and build morale.

☑ I already do this [ ]   I need to revise my approach [ ]

Any of the following needs may govern behaviour, determine motivation, and affect morale.

- **Need for achievement** - motivated by accomplishing something challenging, being better than others, achieving success. These team members respond to opportunities to stretch and test their abilities.

- **Need for power** - motivated by having an impact on situations and exercising leadership and authority. These team members respond to opportunities to make decisions, influence others, and direct projects.

- **Need for affiliation** - motivated by interacting with others, and developing friendly relationships. These team members respond to opportunities for teamwork, helping others, group meetings, and communicating with others.

- **Need for autonomy** - motivated by freedom to act, determining their own priorities, and independence from the supervision and authority of others. These team members respond to opportunities to make their own choices, set their own schedules, work independently of others, and have responsibility for their own actions.

- **Need for esteem** - motivated by recognition, praise, and the acknowledgement, attention, and respect of others. These team members respond to public recognition; status, lots of feedback, and tokens of appreciation for good work.

- **Need for safety and security** - motivated by job security, steady income, hazard-free work environment. These team members respond to jobs with tenure or protection, predictable work, routine, risk-free activities. Salary and benefits may be particularly important.

- **Need for equity** - motivated by having conditions, hours, salary, privileges that are equal to others. May have a strong sense of conscience or ethics. These team members respond to being treated fairly, honestly, and without favouritism.

- **Need for self-actualisation** - motivated by learning and self-development. These team members respond to opportunities for self-expression, self-discovery, and new experiences

31

The leader will need to express personal appreciation for any special effort or achievement.

Any special efforts or achievements which contribute to the team's performance deserve the immediate and open appreciation of the leader. Genuine, but small acknowledgements, such as saying a sincere 'Thank you' or 'Well done' or making and presenting the member with an extra cup of coffee or tea, and making sure everyone knows why, is a most powerful recognition of employee performance. It can increase motivation and improve morale throughout the team by an amount that is out of all proportion to the time and trouble involved. (However, do not allow the employee to use the opportunity to raise other matters, such as a salary increase, time off or such like. If a new topic is raised, set up a separate meeting to discuss it.)

 I already do this [ ] I need to revise my approach [ ]

As leader, you will need to express positive expectations

Even in the most difficult and demanding conditions, you must express your expectations of the team's performance in positive terms. It may be fair and realistic for you to acknowledge that conditions are indeed difficult or demanding, but by stating your expectations in positive terms, you will convey confidence in the members' abilities and commitment, will reinforce motivation and morale, and will be more likely to obtain a positive result.

I already do this [ ] I need to revise my approach [ ]

As leader, you will need to continually monitor members' motivation and morale by observing and listening, and will need to take appropriate action to maintain them at high levels.

It is not appropriate for you to make no response to indications that a member's motivation or morale is lagging, or to take the view that the situation will correct itself given time. Demotivation and poor morale are contagious, and left untreated can seriously undermine team effort and adversely affect results.

Any of the following may be appropriate to the conditions that obtain.

● Ask if the employee has a problem he or she would like to discuss. Be prepared to show genuine interest and make a genuine effort to help. If the problem is personal, deal with it in the strictest confidence

 I already do this [ ] **I need to revise my approach** [ ]

● If you suspect the employee is unhappy about some aspect of work, invite his or her opinion about it. At least you will have the opportunity to correct any misunderstanding, and you may learn something you were not aware of that could be dealt with in a better way.

 I already do this [ ] **I need to revise my approach** [ ]

On a broader scale you may be able to consider any of the following.

● **Job rotation**. It is easier to change jobs than to change people. Someone who has been doing the same job for a long time may no longer be challenged by it. By giving them the opportunity to change jobs you can relieve boredom, increase motivation and morale, and develop a more versatile team member.

 I already do this [ ] **I need to revise my approach** [ ]

● **Job enlargement**. Some employees become frustrated and demotivated if a job is too easy for them or is too simple or too limited in its scope. Adding new responsibilities or expanding the task load, even on a temporary basis to help out another member who is overloaded, will remove the cause of frustration, will increase motivation and morale, and may improve team bonding.

I already do this [ ]   I need to revise my approach [ ]

● **Job enrichment**. Giving some employees more autonomy, or more input into decision making, or more interesting or challenging projects, or whole rather than fragmented tasks can make the job more desirable and satisfying, and can again increase motivation and morale.

 I already do this [ ]   I need to revise my approach [ ]

Internal Relationships

There is always a potential for conflict between team objectives and the personal goals and expectations of individual members. If they are not resolved, interpersonal difficulties may develop and result in poor performance, absenteeism, disruptive behaviour, or even employee turnover.

Some managers see the responsibility for these matters resting somewhere else in the organisation, such as with the Personnel staff. Successful leaders understand that, within their own work unit, it is they themselves who have responsibility for, and benefit from this aspect of people management. By being proactive in this area, they can secure good internal relationships, and improve team bonding, job satisfaction and productivity

☑ **I already do this [ ] I need to revise my approach [ ]**

As leader, you will need to keep members informed of developments within the organisation and will communicate as much as possible.

By holding regular (weekly or fortnightly or monthly) two-way communication sessions with members to pass on all information which is not strictly confidential and to discuss in detail matters that are directly relevant to the team's operation, you can reduce the opportunity for unsettling, uninformed gossip and speculation.

☑ **I already do this [ ] I need to revise my approach [ ]**

Any of the following may be the subject of a two-way communication session.

● **debriefings** - after any important meeting attended, but only covering matters which are not strictly confidential.

☑ **I already do this** [ ] **I need to revise my approach** [ ]

- **information** - about important decisions the leader is taking. People buy into and support and defend decisions if they have taken part in the decision-making process. Where possible team members should be involved in team decisions, but there will be times when the leader needs to take a personal decision on some matter involving the team, and on these occasions should explain the reasons as well as the purpose.

☑ **I already do this** [ ] **I need to revise my approach** [ ]

- **problem solving** - involving members in the problem solving processes (problem identification, solution generation) in matters which affect them or the team operation.

☑ **I already do this** [ ] **I need to revise my approach** [ ]

- **celebrating success** - ensuring members share in the successes of the team. Making sure everyone knows what has been achieved, how it has been achieved, and giving credit where it is due.

☑ **I already do this** [ ] **I need to revise my approach** [ ]

Well-being

The leader will set standards for well-being, will buy into them himself, and will show by his own example the personal effort he expects from team members.

As leader, you should show genuine concern for the well-being of team members.

- You should make a genuine enquiry if a member appears unwell or unhappy, and should try to provide appropriate advice or assistance. Small things, like remembering members' birthdays, or making a kindly enquiry from time to time about a member's family will also emphasise your interest and commitment towards members, will reinforce team bonding, and will build loyalty in return.

 I already do this [ ]   I need to revise my approach [ ]

● You should extend your concern for well-being to matters such as care for personal property, including the property and equipment of the organisation, maintaining an appropriate standard of tidiness and cleanliness in the work area, and compliance with the company's rules and directives on health and safety at work.

 I already do this [ ]   I need to revise my approach [ ]

● You should maintain high standards of care in matters such as personal health, hygiene and dress, and encourage the other team members to do the same

I already do this [ ]   I need to revise my approach [ ]

As leader, you will need to take care of the team's practical needs and protect its reputation.

Team members will expect you to make sure their practical needs are met, that they have the right materials and equipment to do the job, and that additional or replacement resources are anticipated and provided in time to maintain continuity. They will expect that any complaints or criticisms of the team or individual members made by outsiders are promptly investigated.

If complaints or criticisms are justified, prompt remedial action should be taken to rectify the situation with the complainant. If they are unfounded, the situation should be verified with the complainant with equal promptness.

☑ I already do this [ ]   I need to revise my approach [ ]

Conflict management

Some managers are uncomfortable with interpersonal conflict, and will try to avoid or ignore disagreements, or suppress them by adopting an aggressive style of response involving threats or ultimatums. None of these approaches will work to resolve the dispute. Quarrels that are allowed to continue can have an increasingly disruptive effect on work effort, efficiency, and team bonding. Those that are suppressed by threat can fester below the surface, undermining work effort, efficiency, and team bonding, only to break out disruptively again sooner or later.

However, while dealing with conflict is a part of every manager's job, and the effective handling of conflict is an essential component of managerial responsibility, there are many reasons why conflicts develop at work and not all of them are undesirable.

Conflicts can be challenging and enjoyable. Disagreement and debate can promote a better understanding; the give and take of ideas can increase creativity and innovation; challenging decisions rather than rubber-stamping them can make for better decisions; rivalries can stimulate motivation and performance; expressing differences of opinion can challenge complacency and dogma.

On the other hand, a total absence of conflict may indicate stagnated work effort, little concern for efficiency, and poor team commitment.

Whether conflict is evident or not, it will influence performance. The leader's task is to develop that influence in positive ways, to maintain conflict at an acceptable and productive level, and to provide means for resolving it when it causes harm.

The first rule of conflict management is ...

Make sure you know the causes before you make a response.

I already do this [ ] I need to revise my approach [ ]

Any of the following may be the source of conflict:

- interpersonal - differences in attitudes, beliefs, and values

- role delineation, misunderstandings about who does what

- interdependence - one person or group's reliance on another for information, support, materials, etc.

- shared resources, where two or more people or groups share the same resources, e.g. equipment, work area, etc.

- goal differences, where there are different priorities, e.g. the goals for quality may conflict with the goals for output

- differentiation, where different individuals or groups need to operate in different ways, e.g. the approach of the credit control department may need to be very different from that of the sales team, or the time scale for a closely detailed research task may differ substantially from an urgent production one

As leader, you should keep aware of the potential for conflict between members, particularly during times of change and when it is necessary for them to interact with other work groups or departments, and you should establish a personal strategy for resolving conflict.

Some conflict is inevitable when people work as a group, and may require you to intervene to bring the different parties together. The degree of intervention will depend on the extent of the conflict.

 I already do this [ ] I need to revise my approach [ ]

Methods of intervention

● Intervening as a **mediator**, the leader will help clarify the issues, will encourage the parties to co-operate, will set the ground rules for rational discussion, and will act impartially to help the conflicting parties settle their own dispute.

 I already do this [ ]   I need to revise my approach [ ]

●   Intervening as an **arbitrator**, the leader will decide on the issues, will hear both sides, will evaluate the evidence, and will make a decision, binding upon the parties, to settle the dispute.

 I already do this [ ]   I need to revise my approach [ ]

● If the conflict is between the leader and the team or between the leader and a member of the team, it may be necessary to enlist the assistance of an **external mediator** to help clarify the issues.

 I already do this [ ]   I need to revise my approach [ ]

The following are suggested as guidelines for resolving conflict.

● Make sure you know the causes before you make a response. Particularly if things get heated, it is easy for communication to be rushed, to make faulty assumptions, and to jump to conclusions. Take time to ask questions, to listen to statements and answers, and to consider the issues.

 I already do this [ ]   I need to revise my approach [ ]

● Decide whether to act as mediator or arbitrator.

 I already do this [ ]   I need to revise my approach [ ]

● Encourage discussion. Find somewhere where real discussion between the parties can take place under your mediation, and without interference from others. Slow things down, avoid interruptions, allow them to talk, and try to encourage a willingness to listen.

 I already do this [ ]   **I need to revise my approach** [ ]

● Remain objective and co-operative. Keep open-minded, and avoid predetermined impressions. Help each party to clarify their position, and listen carefully for the core complaint or the key area of misunderstanding.

 I already do this [ ]   **I need to revise my approach** [ ]

● Try not to impose a solution. People keep better to decisions they have made for themselves. Particularly in minor disputes, it is better if the parties involved can be guided to their own solution of things.

 I already do this [ ]   **I need to revise my approach** [ ]

● But if you have to arbitrate, deal directly and assertively with the issues and make your decision honestly and ethically.

 I already do this [ ]   **I need to revise my approach** [ ]

Personal Progress Review
Module #1

Start date of Module #1: ____
1st review date:_____ 2nd review date:_____

If you have followed the guidance given in the preceding pages, you should have made valuable progress in developing your management knowledge and skills. To evaluate your progress, you should now complete the following section by marking an assessment on each of the rating scales to show the extent of change evident since the start of this module.

Please remember that this programme is designed to help you develop your management knowledge and skills through self-managed active learning. It is you who will make it work, and you who will benefit. The circumstances of your appointment may not make the same degree of progress possible in every area of activity, and in some you may not, at this stage, have made as much progress as you like. If this is the case, don't mislead yourself by marking above your achievement. Build on what you have done, and try again. You will gain most advantage from your efforts by making your assessment as honestly and realistically as you can.

Team building

On a scale of 1 - 10, where 5 represents the level of previous performance, indicate to what extent you consider the group's performance to have increased or decreased as a result of team-building activities you have introduced.

Decrease   Previously   Increase
After 1 month: [1] [2] [3] [4] [5] [6] [7] [8] [9] [10]
After 2 months: [1] [2] [3] [4] [5] [6] [7] [8] [9] [10]

Developing self-esteem

On a scale of 1 - 10, where 5 represents your estimate of the previous level of members' self-esteem, indicate to what extent you consider the group's self-esteem to have increased or decreased as a result of action you have taken.

Decrease   Previously   Increase

After 1 month: [1] [2] [3] [4] [5] [6] [7] [8] [9] [10]
After 2 months: [1] [2] [3] [4] [5] [6] [7] [8] [9] [10]

Communicating

On a scale of 1 - 10, where 5 represents your estimate of how effective previous communication has been, indicate to what extent you consider the group to be better or worse informed and up to date as a result of action you have taken.

Worse   Previously   Better

After 1 month: [1] [2] [3] [4] [5] [6] [7] [8] [9] [10]
After 2 months: [1] [2] [3] [4] [5] [6] [7] [8] [9] [10]

On a similar scale, where 5 represents your estimate of how well you were previously in touch with and informed about team members' views, needs, and concerns, indicate to what extent you consider your awareness to have increased or decreased as a result of action you have taken.

Decrease   Previously   Increase

After 1 month: [1] [2] [3] [4] [5] [6] [7] [8] [9] [10]
After 2 months: [1] [2] [3] [4] [5] [6] [7] [8] [9] [10]

Gaining commitment

On a scale of 1 - 10, where 5 represents your estimate of how effective previous commitment has been, indicate to what extent you consider members to be more or less able to commit to team objectives as a result of action you have taken.

Less able   Previously   More able

After 1 month: [1] [2] [3] [4] [5] [6] [7] [8] [9] [10]
After 2 months: [1] [2] [3] [4] [5] [6] [7] [8] [9] [10]

Motivation and morale building

On a scale of 1 - 10, where 5 represents your estimate of the previous levels of motivation and morale, indicate to what extent you consider motivation and morale to have increased or decreased as a result of action you have taken.

Decrease   Previously   Increase

After 1 month: [1] [2] [3] [4] [5] [6] [7] [8] [9] [10]
After 2 months: [1] [2] [3] [4] [5] [6] [7] [8] [9] [10]

Internal relationships

On a scale of 1 - 10, where 5 represents your estimate of the previous quality of internal relationships, indicate to what extent you consider these to have been improved or impaired as a result of action you have taken.

Impaired   Previously   Improved

After 1 month: [1] [2] [3] [4] [5] [6] [7] [8] [9] [10]
After 2 months: [1] [2] [3] [4] [5] [6] [7] [8] [9] [10]

Well-being

On a scale of 1 - 10, where 5 represents your estimate of the previous state of well-being within the team, indicate to what extent you consider it to have been improved or impaired as a result of action you have taken.

Impaired   Previously   Improved

After 1 month: [1] [2] [3] [4] [5] [6] [7] [8] [9] [10]

After 2 months: [1] [2] [3] [4] [5] [6] [7] [8] [9] [10]

Conflict management

On a scale of 1 - 10, where 5 represents your estimate of the previous effectiveness of conflict management, indicate to what extent you consider it has been improved or worsened as a result of action you have taken.

Worsened   Previously   Improved

After 1 month: [1] [2] [3] [4] [5] [6] [7] [8] [9] [10]

After 2 months: [1] [2] [3] [4] [5] [6] [7] [8] [9] [10]

END OF MODULE #1

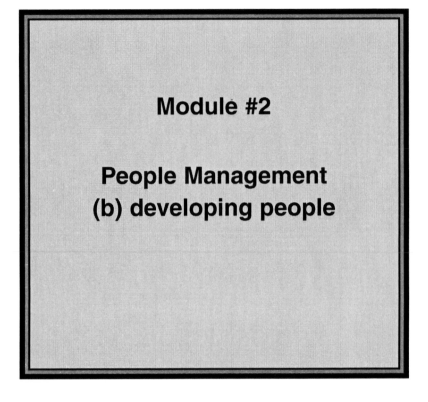

Module #2

**People Management
(b) developing people**

Start date for this module _____

Skills Assessment and Training

Making sure that people can do their jobs effectively is a key area of managerial responsibility. Some of this will follow as a response to information obtained from the formal Annual Performance Review, and the sensible manager will use this information as the basis for planning and developing manpower strategies for the medium and longer term. However, some of it will arise from the need to respond to more immediate situations. These may come from the day-to-day application of pre-planned strategies, but may also involve arrangements to cover unplanned circumstances, such as new or changed items of work, new or changed equipment or processes, inducting new employees, or reallocating tasks owing to employee absence or turnover.

Dealing with these requirements may create conditions where the existing knowledge and skills of some employees are not wholly adequate and may need to be upgraded, or it may require some employees to develop new knowledge and new skills. In either event, it is, of course, not appropriate to wait until the next Annual Performance Review before deciding what to do, and the manager needs to be able to make a response based on having a current understanding of each person's relevant knowledge and skills in the job, and being able to provide any necessary assistance where areas of knowledge or skill require improvement.

In very simple terms, the manager needs to know on an ongoing basis:

- does the employee know what he is doing and why?
- does the employee have the necessary skills at an acceptable level?
- what assistance does the employee need to do the job better or to meet new or changed job requirements?
- could the employee give assistance to others to upgrade their knowledge or skills?

47

In very simple terms, the employee needs to know on an ongoing basis:

- am I doing what I'm supposed to be doing?
- am I doing it well enough?
- what help can I get to do my job better?

There are many methods of assessment, each with its own merits, but for the purpose of this programme, most are too complex, take too long to set up, take too long to produce results, and make too much demand on the manager's time to be used on an ongoing basis.

The following two pages set out an easy way of assessing employee knowledge and skills.

- It requires very little setting up.
- It is easily understood and applied.
- It is specific to individuals and individual jobs.
- It gives an easily verified indication of knowledge and skills.
- It can be rapidly adjusted to new or changed job requirements.
- It accesses help to individuals and teams, and supports team bonding.
- It makes little demand on the manager's time.
- It is not intended to replace the Annual Performance Review, but to operate within the manpower strategies which are developed from the APR, and to support them on an ongoing basis.

DEVELOPMENT SUPPORT REVIEW
SELF-RATED ASSESSMENT

Name: _____ Date: / /

The purpose of this review is to find out what help or training you might need to improve your own job performance, or might be able to give to others as part of team development support activities.

Decide which are the key activities of your job, and write them into the table below.

N.B. The Review form makes provision for six key job activities. This will be sufficient for most jobs, but if you consider that your job has more than six key activities, decide which are the six most important activities and list only these.

Using the following scale of values in which 3 is the benchmark level of skill required, place a check mark [✓] in the appropriate box to enter your own assessment of your ability to carry out the tasks involved. Please be realistic in your assessment. If you need training or assistance, or can give training or assistance to others, this is your opportunity to say so.

Value 1:   I do not have enough knowledge or skill to carry out the task involved, and urgently need training or assistance

Value 2:   I know what needs to be done, but still find it difficult, and would welcome further training or assistance

Value 3:   I have adequate knowledge and skill to carry out the task involved, and do not need further training or assistance at present

Value 4:   I have a high level of knowledge and skill in the task involved, and would be prepared to assist or train others.

Values

Key job activity	1	2	3	4

Additional notes or comment:

Using the Development Support Review

The Development Support Review can be used at any time where there is need for a rapid, informal, and easily verified means of assessing job knowledge and skill.

By adopting self-assessment as its basis, the review enables you to obtain valuable information about an employee's knowledge and skills in key job activities without becoming tied up in a lengthy process of administration. The employee completes a photocopy of the Review form while you get on with other things.

For on-going assessments of existing staff members

The employee should be asked to complete the Review form by writing in the key activities of the job, and marking in his own rating of his ability to carry out the tasks involved according to the values given on the form. Remember, this is a self-assessment review, and it is important that the employee completes the form without any assistance from the manager.

Nothing is more certain to defeat the purpose of this Review, so far as existing staff members are concerned, than an imposed review of performance in areas of activity which are not held to be, or are not understood to be, essential to the purpose of the job by the people who perform it.

● **By writing in the key activities, the employee will indicate his understanding of which activities are most essential to the job's purpose.**

Checking these entries against a current Job Description, or against an interim task or project instruction if appropriate, will enable the manager to see if the employee really knows what the job is about, what key tasks are involved, and will show where discussion is needed to clear any misunderstandings or uncertainties about its purpose or key activities.

● **By marking in a value rating against each key activity, the**

51

employee will indicate how well he believes he is able to carry out the tasks involved.

Checking these entries against actual results, or by simply watching the employee carry out the tasks involved, will enable the manager to see if the self-assessed skill ratings are realistic, and will show where assistance or training is needed to support the individual or, if appropriate, how the individual could provide assistance or training to support the team.

For reviewing recently inducted staff members, or recently introduced new or changed working practices.

The new staff member or the new or changed working practices should be allowed to settle in for a short time, perhaps one or two weeks, before using the Development Support Review.

In order to reinforce a new employee's understanding of the job's purpose and task requirements, or to reinforce new or changed working practices, it may be necessary for the manager to help the employee to specify which are the key job activities.

However, it should be left to the employee to mark in a value rating against each key activity. Again, checking these entries against actual results, or by simply watching the employee carry out the tasks involved, will enable the manager to see if the self-assessed skill ratings are realistic, and will show where assistance or training is needed to support the individual.

Where performance in recently introduced new or changed working practices is being assessed, the value ratings may highlight unforeseen snags and show where adjustments are needed to improve their effectiveness.

Keeping in touch and informed

On an even less formal basis, there is another way for the manager to obtain an extensive range of need-to-know

information about individual employee's knowledge, skills, and training needs, and about the overall effectiveness of team performance.

Generally referred to as 'Management by walking about', it is the traditional method through which by observation and discussion, by keeping involved and aware, and by taking and showing a genuine interest in employees' activities, the manager can keep in touch, informed, and abreast of developments.

The performance objective is for employees to do their jobs effectively, to keep their activities progressing on schedule, and to contribute knowledge and skill to the best of their ability. The manager will need to know how well this is being done, and if assistance or training is necessary.

There is, however, a fine line between taking and showing a genuine interest in employees' activities and being officious. While employees are likely to welcome genuine interest, will appreciate an opportunity to discuss a particular problem, and will accept sincere advice, they may be disconcerted if they feel they have become the focus of too much attention.

Employees should be encouraged to get on with their jobs without either feeling constrained by needless intrusion by their boss, or developing an unnecessary reliance on the boss's say so before taking action. While it is important for the manager to maintain contact, it should be no more than is actually necessary.

[See also the section on Empowerment later in this Module.]

Improving performance

Where there is an evident need for an employee to improve performance, the manager will be better able to respond by following a logical decision-making process to define which action will be most appropriate.

The following is suggested as a suitable decision-making structure.

- **First, establish the problem and its causes.**
Performance loss may be the result of inadequate job knowledge or job skills, but there can be many other causes, such as health concerns and other personal problems, relationship difficulties at work or at home, equipment problems, work overloads, or even boredom and frustration. [Cross check with Module #1, section: Motivation and Building Morale]

 I already do this [ ]   I need to revise my approach [ ]

- **Second, decide whether to provide assistance or training.**
It is usually fairly obvious which of the causes can be dealt with by assistance and perhaps even better by discussion and counselling, and which will require training, but it will be advisable to confirm the situation with the employee concerned before deciding which course to pursue.
[Cross check with Module #1, section: Conflict Management]

 I already do this [ ]   I need to revise my approach [ ]

- **Third, decide which form the assistance or training should take. What will give the best result?**

 I already do this [ ]   I need to revise my approach [ ]

Where assistance is indicated, it may mean arranging time off for the employee to visit a doctor or other specialist for advice about health or other personal concerns, it may mean stepping in to mediate in an interpersonal conflict, or it may mean making practical arrangements to help with a work overload or equipment difficulties. In any such cases, it is important for the manager to act, and the action should be seen to be made as a positive commitment to relieving the employee's difficulties and improving their level of performance.

I already do this [ ]   I need to revise my approach [ ]

Where training or retraining in particular areas of job knowledge or job skills is indicated, there are several options to consider, and the choice taken will depend on the level of improvement required and the type of learning needed.

One-to-one coaching. This is a very practical form of on-the-job training, where someone with appropriate knowledge, ability, and experience provides instruction and guidance in task activities and dealing with problems, and facilitates the improvements in job knowledge and job skills by goal-setting and feedback

It has the benefits of being able to be tailored to here-and-now, quickly arranged, applied on a local basis, and aimed at individual needs. It is supportive to team bonding, and easily monitored by the manager.

It has the disadvantage of taking a more productive employee away from his own activities to provide the coaching. This should be a temporary arrangement, and each coaching session should be for a fixed period of time, but it needs to be properly planned and controlled.

Self-managed learning. For certain purposes with certain people, self-managed learning can be very effective. It can be applied in different ways. Self-paced manuals such as user manuals for computers, DIY-based individual instruction workbooks, audio cassettes, and video tapes are all forms of self-managed learning.

It has the benefits of providing learning by experience within the particular context of the learner's job requirements in a way that allows for the learner's individuality. It progresses at a pace suited to the learner, and enables the learning process to be fitted around other work demands or even during free time.

It has the disadvantage of relying on the learner's commitment which can lessen over time unless there is a built in arrangement requiring evidence of progress at staged intervals. There is little human interaction for those who learn best with the direct assistance of others, and it is not so quickly arranged as one-to-one coaching. Some of these disadvantages can be discounted by the appointment of a Mentor.

In-house training. Internal training departments can often provide valuable assistance in providing or finding the training that managers need for their subordinates. They may have specialist training skills in the area required, may have an appropriately prepared training programme, may have the right equipment and environment for rapid learning, or may know where these things can be obtained.

They have the benefit of being able to concentrate time and attention on the training required, of being able to provide training that employs a 'company' language and 'company' terms, that maintains a 'company' culture, and supports the 'company' aims and policies.

They have the disadvantage of being demand regulated. Except in larger organisations, in-house training may not be an available option, and even large training departments do not always have expertise in all training topics. What they provide is usually determined by what is most in demand, for example, the training department in an organisation that manufactures mechanical handling equipment may have no expertise in financial management procedures. There is also the question of whether their schedule will enable them to provide the training as and when it is needed.

Public seminars. These may include programmes run by trade or employers' organisations, professional training companies, management consultants, individual speakers, or courses sponsored by universities, colleges, or vocational schools.

They have the benefit of offering a wide diversity of topics, facilitators, and cost. They usually disseminate knowledge and information that is at the forefront of current thinking. They allow employees to meet people from other companies, and hear about the experience of other organisations

They have the disadvantage of having to meet the needs of participants from various levels, functions, and types of organisations. They must be general rather than specific in their coverage, and some or much of the content may simply not be applicable in some cases. There is also the possibility that in having discussion with participants from other organisations, sensitive company information may be disclosed.

Outside providers. These are trainers or consultants with specialist knowledge brought in to create a programme that meets unique training needs. They can deliver the programme, or prepare a programme for someone in the company to deliver, or train someone to deliver the training in subsequent sessions after presentation of the initial session.

They have the advantage of being able to tailor the training to specific needs, and provide objectivity and credibility. They usually disseminate knowledge and information that is at the forefront of current thinking. They can be brought in to provide training as and when it is needed, and may be the best solution where the training is a politically sensitive issue.

They have the disadvantage of needing time to design an appropriately tailored programme and its materials.

● Fourth, decide who should provide it.

It is the manager's responsibility to provide employees with the assistance and training necessary to improve performance. This does not mean that the manager must do all the assisting and training himself, and the options listed above should be considered in each case before deciding which form of training is likely to best meet the employee's needs and produce the required improvements.

It is also necessary to consider the question of cost. There will be fees if a public seminar or outside provider is to be involved. There will also be an actual cost if training is provided by an in-house facility, and in the time trainees will spend away from the job, and there may also be travel expenses. These considerations will need to be taken into account and may, in the end, be determined by the extent of an available budget allowance.

It is not easy to make an advance assessment of costs against the benefits training can provide, but it should be possible to see if costs are justified after training is completed. Areas in which there should be some tangible benefit obtained should not only include better productivity, and better attention to detail and quality, but may also include better morale, fewer disputes or grievances, fewer signs of stress, reduced absenteeism, and fewer complaints from customers or internal 'clients'. Where these are obtained, it can be safely assumed that not only was the training effective, but it was worth the cost.

Performance standards and goal setting

In his own work, as well as in his expectations of performance from subordinates, the manager should be an advocate of excellence, and should maintain an ongoing team-wide commitment to improving performance standards and performance goals.

There are three basic methods of controlling performance standards and developing performance goals - Quality-control Systems, Quality Circles, and Two-way Commitment Links. Of these three, Two-way Commitment Links are likely to be the most appropriate and the most effective where the number of employees is relatively small and the manager is able to maintain a personal involvement with the individual employee. For comparison, brief details of the other two methods are also given below.

Quality-control systems

These were developed initially in volume production manufacturing industries to pick up and correct the worst defects and faults in the work of low-skill, low-paid production-line employees. They were an attempt cut out errors in production that could result in product recalls or replacements, consumer actions, or lost customers and the potentially exorbitant costs involved. They did manage to deal with the worst production-line defects and faults, but did nothing to improve either the skill or the pay of the employees, and therefore had little to do with developing a culture of excellence.

Far from improving standards, Quality-control systems can undermine quality. If an employee knows that a quality-control inspector will check his work and correct any errors, omissions, or faults found, it is very likely that he will soon become complacent and careless about quality standards.

Certainly such a system provides no incentive for the employee to improve, and the introduction of a quality-control inspector severs the vital two-way commitment link that should exist between the employee and his manager.

Quality Circles

The successor to Quality-control systems; these involve small groups of workers, typically three to twelve members, from the same department or work area who voluntarily meet together for about an hour per week in paid time to identify, analyse, and solve work-related problems. They present their solutions to management and, in some cases implement them themselves, working under a trained circle leader who is usually an employee at Supervisor level.

The system involves cooperation between members in the group, but requires to be formally set up within the organisation's operating structure, formally supported by management, formally prepared for by training in QC procedures, and formally run with well-defined objectives. While Quality Circles encourage employees to a greater commitment to excellence than Quality-control systems, they make only a partial contribution to the vital two-way commitment link that should exist between the employee and his manager, and work best in large organisations where the numbers of people employed makes it difficult for managers to maintain close communication and contact with individuals.

Two-way Commitment Links

These build on the relationship that exists between the manager and each individual employee. Through this, the employee is encouraged to be personally responsible for the excellence of his work, to do it properly to prevent errors, and omissions, and to spot his own mistakes and put them right.

The manager shows commitment by promoting an agenda for excellence:

- that involves the employee in defining the standards required (these should be for every aspect of the job and in quantifiable terms wherever possible)
- that expresses an expectation that the employee will achieve the standards required and agreed

- that examines the reasons for any failure to achieve the standards required, is critical of error or omission, but is patient with improvement
- that provides any necessary training and equipment for the employee to achieve the standards required
- that acknowledges the employee's achievement of the standards required or improvements towards them (examples of excellence can serve as models for others)
- that stimulates the employee's involvement and maintains a format of achievement, improvement, and re-achievement by having standards re-defined to create a cycle of activity through which the emphasis on quality becomes perpetual.

 I already do this [ ]   I need to revise my approach [ ]

The employee is encouraged to show commitment by being given conditions that will enable him to buy into quality standards, will support his efforts, acknowledge his progress, and provide an incentive to improve.

Goal setting

Given that the employee knows what he has to do, has received appropriate training, and has at least the basic knowledge and skills required, the next step is to establish standards of performance which allow the manager and the employee to evaluate how well the job is being done in each if its key result areas i.e. those parts of the job in which the employee is expected to act. From there, they will be able to agree new objectives that will reinforce commitment to the job and encourage improvement in future performance.

It is imperative that employees know the precise standards they are expected to achieve, and is unfair to hold them accountable for performance requirements that are vague or unknown. It is therefore necessary to discuss these requirements with each individual and to set performance standards that are specific to each key result area for the individual person concerned. (Employees are usually better motivated to achieve standards when they have been involved in setting them.) Once agreed, the performance standards effectively become the set goals which the employee is expected to achieve.

☑ **I already do this** [ ] **I need to revise my approach** [ ]

To be effective, goals should have the following characteristics, which produce the acronym **SMART**.

Specific: the employee should be able to clearly understand what is expected

Measurable: goals should be quantifiable, and the employee should be able to assess progress towards goals on an ongoing basis

Attainable, but challenging - goals should involve some element of challenge to motivate the employee towards attainable, but better performance

Relevant: goals should be related to the key result areas

Time-oriented: goals should be related to time scales.

Most performance can be measured in terms of quantity, quality, time or cost. If, for some reason, the standard of performance cannot be expressed in measurable terms, for example a personal skill such as communication, it should still be possible to describe in its essential requirements the standard of performance expected.

Since goals can be raised as employees' skills improve, reviewing performance standards as part of a Two-way Commitment Link can progressively and effectively develop a culture of excellence when repeated over time. Maintaining the process enables the manager to ensure that standards don't drop and bad habits don't creep in.

☑ **I already do this** [ ] **I need to revise my approach** [ ]

Empowerment

'As we look ahead into the next century, leaders will be those who empower others. Empowering leadership means bringing out the energy and capabilities that people have, and getting them to work together in a way they wouldn't do otherwise.
That requires that they see the positive impact they can have and sense the opportunities.'
Bill Gates, Chairman and CEO, Microsoft Corporation

Empowerment is about creating an environment that fosters the involvement, development, and growth of people by pushing responsibilities for action and decision-making downwards to the persons taking the action. It means that people have the opportunity to become more involved in the actions and decisions that affect them. As a result, they can feel more ownership in the processes, can become more committed to achieving their objectives, and can develop a self-expectation of greater productivity and improved standards of performance.

The traditional concept of management meant top-end planning, organising, directing, and controlling. To some managers, empowerment may indicate losing these areas of authority and power, running the operation like a democracy, and they may feel threatened by it.

However, the empowering concept does not mean that the manager relinquishes control, or authority, or power, or simply hands over the running of the operation to subordinates.

It is about creating the conditions in which subordinates have more freedom to act and initiate without always having to seek approval, in return for accepting more responsibility for their actions and decisions. But at all times the manager remains in control, sustaining authority, and running the operation in response to its business commitments.

For these conditions to apply, the aspects of work for which empowerment is being introduced need to be clearly understood and agreed upon by the manager and the employee concerned. It will help if these are recorded in writing.

A useful start for this is a list of the key activities contained in the employee's area of work. (Check these out with the same type of Grid used in the Review of Key Team Activities: Module #1). The list of items obtained will provide a framework from within which the empowerment parameters can be developed to produce a brief, but clear record of empowerment conditions including:

- task objectives
- areas of accountability
- expected standards of performance
- limits of authority.

As with other management initiatives, empowerment doesn't just happen, but needs to be introduced, and can be introduced only if certain conditions apply. Use the following checklist to verify if they apply in each case, and only proceed if you are satisfied the circumstances will allow you to do so successfully.

Checklist of readiness for empowerment

Tick as appropriate using the following status values
1: ready now 2: some development needed 3: major development needed

Required condition	Status
Empowerment requires a shift in attitude from a hierarchical, top-down chain of command operation to one involving shared personal accountability.	1 2 3 [ ] [ ] [ ]
It requires the manager to show a lead by involving subordinates in the planning and organising of activities in which they are directly involved.	[ ] [ ] [ ]
It requires the manager to trust people to take actions and decisions without always referring back to him for approval.	[ ] [ ] [ ]
It requires the manager to set guidelines and boundaries for	

subordinates' actions and decisions without stifling their ability
to take initiatives and get problems solved.   [ ] [ ] [ ]

It requires a report structure that enables the manager to remain
informed, and therefore in control, without tying subordinates up in
excessive documentation.   [ ] [ ] [ ]

It requires a willingness to take some risk by giving people
additional responsibility, but in a way that makes success more
likely than failure -
  • by giving specific instructions
  • by making sure they have the knowledge and training required
  • by regularly following up without communicating lack of trust   [ ] [ ] [ ]

It requires all subordinates to accept accountability for
  empowered behaviour, and the consequences of their actions
  and decisions   [ ] [ ] [ ]

It requires recognition that some people may need additional help
  and encouragement to accept empowered behaviour, and that some
  may not be able to accept the personal responsibilities involved, even
  after extensive coaching, and may be better employed in another
  role or another department.   [ ] [ ] [ ]

It requires everyone involved to understand that empowerment is **not** -
  • a free-for-all system where people do what they want and decide
    their own boundaries
  • a democracy where everyone gets an equal vote on every decision and
    action
  • taking actions and decisions without responsibility for the consequences
    or regard for their effects on others
  • blaming others and making excuses if things go wrong   [ ] [ ] [ ]

Empowerment can follow on naturally from team development
activities, and is easier to introduce where there is already an
established team environment. The manager should expect to see
changes and improvements in employee performance as a result of its
introduction, and should review the conditions under which it
operates if these are not forthcoming.

The benefits that should be identifiable include:
- a more committed workforce
- increased productivity
- better quality work done over sustained periods of time
- more accountability and initiative from employees
- higher levels of cooperation and teamwork
- employees expressing more job satisfaction
- more time for the manager to focus on broader needs.

Delegation

Delegation and empowerment are not different sides of the same coin, but are the same coin purchasing different things. Where empowerment can secure improvements in department performance by developing peoples' abilities to do their own jobs and handle their own responsibilities, delegation can secure improvements in management performance by developing peoples' abilities to take on new jobs and handle new responsibilities.

By developing peoples' abilities to take on new jobs and handle new responsibilities, the manager obtains two significant advantages from delegation.

- It releases the manager from time-consuming repetitive or detailed tasks that could be done by someone else, and creates time that can be used to deal with more pressing matters.
- It enriches the work of subordinates, and helps prepare them for advancement.

Relevant steps to be taken in delegation include the following.

- **Analyse current tasks and identify which ones can be delegated.** Routine, programmed, or fact finding tasks, or the implementation of decisions already taken are the easiest to delegate, and it is better to delegate a whole task than part of one.

I already do this [ ]   I need to revise my approach [ ]

- **Select subordinates** who have demonstrated a willingness to take on more responsibility, and have the right skills, confidence, and motivation. If necessary, prepare the person with special coaching or off-the-job training.

 I already do this [ ]   I need to revise my approach [ ]

- **Define the task** and why it needs to be done, and reassure the person of your faith in their ability to do it. If it requires an increase in responsibility, but does not involve an increase in pay, you may need to show how it will prepare the person for future opportunities.

 I already do this [ ]   I need to revise my approach [ ]

- **Only delegate a vital task when you can be sure it can be done on time and to the required standard.**

 I already do this [ ]   I need to revise my approach [ ]

- **Discuss the deadline**, the standard required, the resources available (budget, equipment, staff), and the location.

 I already do this [ ]   I need to revise my approach [ ]

- **Discuss the authority** the person is being given to make decisions (it should be enough to complete the job), types of problem that must be referred back, any progress reports required, and the form of any final report and/or recommendations to be submitted

 I already do this [ ]   I need to revise my approach [ ]

- **Make feedback on progress routine** at regular intervals, and allocate specific times to go through development together. Apart from this, leave the people to get on with the job.
  - They may make mistakes, but should be given the opportunity to correct them, and should know they can contact you for assistance at any time.
  - They may do things differently, but resist the tendency to insist that things should be done 'your way'. By having some freedom to act, subordinates may find better ways to solve old problems.

 I already do this [ ]   I need to revise my approach [ ]

- **Acknowledge and reward success** appropriately, but don't fail to criticise if necessary, and do not accept work which is incomplete or below the required standards. To do so will not help the subordinate to develop.

 I already do this [ ]   I need to revise my approach [ ]

Disciplines

The disciplines referred to in this section are not those formally established in the Company's Rules of Conduct and Disciplinary Procedures, but the local measures that managers can take to maintain morale, commitment, and continuity of performance as part of an employee development initiative.

Employees find it comfortable to be part of a disciplined work force, and perform better where there is some regulation in the way things are done. By developing a disciplined workforce, managers develop employee effectiveness, and provide themselves with an operational asset.

Steps that can be taken include the following.

- **State clear objectives.** Employees need to have an aim and purpose for their activities before they can he expected to put in effort and commitment

 I already do this [ ]   I need to revise my approach [ ]

- **Maintain effective work programmes and schedules.** Identify the order in which activities will take place, who will be responsible for them, and fix stage dates and completion deadlines.

 I already do this [ ]   I need to revise my approach [ ]

- **Establish shared values.** Take a lead in setting value on responsiveness, enthusiasm, cooperation, support, and openness between employees as well as on individual effort and ability. Demonstrate these qualities in your contact with subordinates, and express clear approval for those who contribute and clear disapproval for those who don't.

 I already do this [ ]   I need to revise my approach [ ]

- **Establish 'good colleague' behaviour**. Take a lead in setting value on courtesy, respect, and appreciation between employees by showing these qualities in your contact with subordinates, and by expressing clear approval for those who comply and clear disapproval for those who don't.

☑ **I already do this [ ]   I need to revise my approach [ ]**

- **Keep involved**. Don't interfere, but keep in touch and aware of developments. Be on hand to advise, be prepared to criticise constructively, and above all be ready to support and encourage.

☑ **I already do this [ ]   I need to revise my approach [ ]**

- **Don't overplay rules**. In general terms, local rules should be kept to an absolute minimum. While you need to show firmness in your expectations of performance and behaviour, remember that employees work best when they feel trusted to get things done.

    Where circumstances make it necessary for local rules to be made, the following conditions should apply:
    - they should be as few in number as possible
    - they should not be unduly restrictive
    - they should not be discriminatory
    - they should be reasonable in content
    - they should be known and understood
    - they should be acceptable and enforceable
    - they should be fair and consistently applied.

☑ **I already do this [ ]   I need to revise my approach [ ]**

Controls

The controls dealt with in this section are those that enable the manager to maintain the direction of activities, that provide continuous information about how well employees are performing against set objectives, and that indicate where further development of employee knowledge or skills is appropriate, or where some remedial action is necessary.

Managing an operational unit without controls is tantamount to driving a car without hands on the steering wheel. In order to ensure that activities are progressing in the direction required to meet objectives, it is essential for the manager to introduce appropriate controls at an early stage. However, controls, like rules, should be as few in number as is consistent with maintaining operational direction and effectiveness

Setting up controls entails the setting up of standards, which then determine measures for performance, and provide guide lines for improving employees' knowledge and skills and increasing general efficiency. Additionally:

- **Controls assist the communication of information and ideas**, help to achieve coordination, and can assist the expansion of employees' knowledge.
- **Controls can fix authority and responsibility** to assist successful delegation
- **Controls provide feedback of information** that can indicate how well instructions, proposals, and policies are being interpreted and applied.
- **Controls can help to identify trends**, and where changes could be considered to improve responsiveness to operational demands.

In general terms, controls work best if built into operating procedures in ways which can be seen as sensible components of the activities involved rather than imposed as external additions to them. They also need to be as least intrusive as possible to the purpose of the activities so that employees can concentrate their time and efforts on achieving objectives rather than responding to controls. Therefore the method of control used will depend on the activity involved as well as the extent of the information required. Different methods that could be selected include the following.

- **Visual and personal:** informal local visual checking of work
- **Reporting:** formal use of regular reports, e.g. daily report of cash flow; weekly report of production output; monthly report of income and profit, etc.
- **Exceptions:** e.g. within credit control, instead of listing all debtors, list only those exceeding a fixed credit limit or a fixed time allowance
- **Rules and regulations:** usually policy related, such as attendance report; time-keeping log; holiday list; conduct record, etc.
- **Systems:** systemising activities with some form of control incorporated into their normal application, e.g. a condition which must be met before the activity can proceed, etc.
- **Ad hoc decisions:** checking response to unplanned incidents to obtain some element of control.

While controls can provide valuable information, they have to be carefully applied. If not, they can be regressive and may involve an unjustified cost. For example, where traditionally businesses used time clocks and clocking-in cards to control employee attendance, many found that control of attendance was more effectively achieved through better local management; by securing better commitment through empowerment and delegation; and the introduction of more flexible working methods which enabled employees to consider themselves participants in the enterprise and valued for their abilities rather than simply being paid for their time. Clocking-in, which had long been regarded as an irksome and demeaning control by most employees, not only became regressive to these developments, but the information it provided was just not worth the time and cost involved, and for those reasons it was justifiably abandoned.

The following general principles about controls are given as guidance.

- **Controls should be part of a common purpose**, e.g. control of staff numbers should be integrated with financial controls, i.e. with what can be afforded

☑ I already do this [ ]   I need to revise my approach [ ]

- **Controls should be sufficiently flexible** to allow for changes in circumstance.

 I already do this [ ]   **I need to revise my approach** [ ]

- **Controls should be simple and easy to understand.** If too complicated and detailed they may fail in their purpose.

 I already do this [ ]   **I need to revise my approach** [ ]

- **Controls must be essential**, otherwise they are simply a pointless exercise in power and may be counter-productive and time-wasting.

 I already do this [ ]   **I need to revise my approach** [ ]

- **Controls must accord with, reflect, and support the policies of the organisation.**

 I already do this [ ]   **I need to revise my approach** [ ]

- **Controls must be in the right quantity.** Too many can be irksome to employees, can undermine morale, initiative, and loyalty, can take up too much of the manager's and employees' time, and can involve needless cost. Too few can mean that the manager does not really know what is happening, and is unable to meet the operational needs of the business or the development needs of employees. It is important to get the balance right.

 I already do this [ ]   **I need to revise my approach** [ ]

Personal Progress Review
Module #2

Start date of Module #2: ____
1st review date:_____ **2nd review date:**_____

If you have followed the guidance given in the preceding pages, you should have made valuable progress in developing your management knowledge and skills. To evaluate your progress, you should now complete the following section by marking an assessment on each of the rating scales to show the extent of change evident since the start of this module.

Please remember that this programme is designed to help you develop your management knowledge and skills through self-managed active learning. It is you who will make it work, and you who will benefit. The circumstances of your appointment may not make the same degree of progress possible in every area of activity, and in some you may not, at this stage, have made as much progress as you like. If this is the case, don't mislead yourself by marking above your achievement. Build on what you have done, and try again. You will gain most advantage from your efforts by making your assessment as honestly and realistically as you can.

Skills assessment and training

On a scale of 1 - 10, where 5 represents your assessment of the overall previous levels of knowledge and skills, indicate to what extent you consider employees' knowledge and skills have improved or worsened as a result of action you have taken.

Worsened   Previously   Improved
After 1 month: [1] [2] [3] [4] [5] [6] [7] [8] [9] [10]
After 2 months: [1] [2] [3] [4] [5] [6] [7] [8] [9] [10]

Performance standards and goal setting

On a scale of 1 - 10, where 5 represents your estimate of the previous effectiveness of performance standards and goal setting, indicate to what extent you consider this to have increased or decreased as a result of action you have taken.

              Decrease   Previously   Increase

After 1 month: [1] [2] [3] [4] [5] [6] [7] [8] [9] [10]

After 2 months: [1] [2] [3] [4] [5] [6] [7] [8] [9] [10]

Empowerment

On a scale of 1 - 10, where 5 represents your estimate of the previous level of employee involvement and commitment, indicate to what extent you consider this to have increased or decreased as a result of action you have taken.

              Decrease   Previously   Increase

After 1 month: [1] [2] [3] [4] [5] [6] [7] [8] [9] [10]

After 2 months: [1] [2] [3] [4] [5] [6] [7] [8] [9] [10]

Delegation

On a scale of 1 - 10, where 5 represents your estimate of the effectiveness of previous delegation, indicate to what extent you consider this to have improved or worsened as a result of action you have taken.

              Worsened   Previously   Improved

After 1 month: [1] [2] [3] [4] [5] [6] [7] [8] [9] [10]

After 2 months: [1] [2] [3] [4] [5] [6] [7] [8] [9] [10]

Disciplines

On a scale of 1 - 10, where 5 represents your estimate of the previous level of work force discipline, indicate to what extent you consider this to have improved or worsened as a result of action you have taken.

Worsened   Previously   Improved

After 1 month: [1] [2] [3] [4] [5] [6] [7] [8] [9] [10]

After 2 months: [1] [2] [3] [4] [5] [6] [7] [8] [9] [10]

Controls

On a scale of 1 - 10, where 5 represent your estimate of the effectiveness of previous controls, indicate to what extent you consider the position to have improved or worsened as a result of action you have taken.

Worsened   Previously   Improved

After 1 month: [1] [2] [3] [4] [5] [6] [7] [8] [9] [10]

After 2 months: [1] [2] [3] [4] [5] [6] [7] [8] [9] [10]

END OF MODULE #2

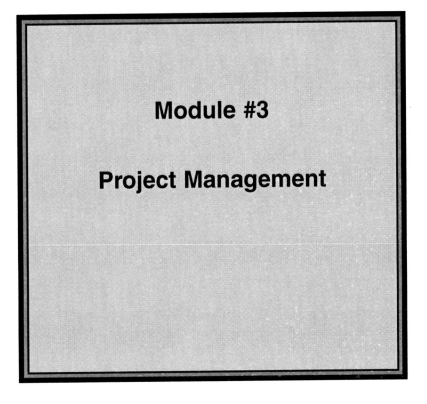

Module #3

Project Management

Start date for this module _____

Project Management

Introduction

This section deals with the local management of operational projects within one functional area, and is not intended to cover in detail the more complex management of strategic projects involving cross-functional activities in different parts of a business's activities. While there are sophisticated computerised project management software applications available for those whose appointments require an extensive involvement in those areas of management, these guidance notes provide a straightforward method of project management that covers the same ground in simpler terms and in a readily accessible form that can be applied effectively in most situations likely to be encountered in local management.

All projects, whether operational or strategic, are structured around three principal areas of management involvement. The degree of involvement may differ from project to project, but the principal areas on which the project is structured remain the same in all cases. These are:

- **Planning**; in which the purpose, scope, resources, requirements, and objectives are decided.
- **Managing**: in which activities are initiated, progress is tracked, and problems are dealt with.
- Concluding; in which results are recorded and assessed, and plans and progress are reviewed to analyse what went right or wrong to assist future project management.

Planning a project

Planning is the first principal area of project management. It establishes the purpose and scope of activities, creates a framework for co-ordinating action, identifies resources, requirements, and objectives, provides a basis on which decisions are made, and defines a structure for controls. It does, therefore, have a direct effect on the eventual success or failure of the project concerned.

There are general principles which apply to planning. These are:

- **Planning requires a clear objective.** You need to clear about what you intend to achieve. This will enable you to define the activities, and objectives of the project and set dates for its commencement and completion.

- **Planning requires an accurate assessment of the present position.** You not only need to be clear about what you intend to achieve, but will also need to be clear about where you are starting from, what you are staring with, and any matters or difficulties that need to be dealt with before your intended activities begin.

- **Planning must always be for the right length of time.** Some guidance on this will come from making a sensible assessment of what is realistically achievable, and whether planning should be strategic or operational. (See below)

- **Planning must be in the right amount of detail.** It is not possible to state precisely what detail will be required, but as a general rule, there must be sufficient detail for everyone involved to understand what is intended and what they will be required to do.

- **All possible courses of action must be considered.** Continually ask yourself, 'Is there a better way?' and 'What would happen if

...?' Try to define alternatives, they not only give you an opportunity to weigh the possibilities of one course of action against another, but will enable you to be assured that your proposals will achieve intended objectives in the most effective, and where possible, the most cost efficient way

- **Planning requires an evaluation of the resources required.** You will need to calculate the financial, technological, administrative, and human resources required to achieve the objectives.

- **Planning must be based on facts.** Don't rely on 'gut feel' or opinions or hearsay. You need to know what the realities are, and can only safely base your proposals on what is known for certain.

- **Planning therefore needs the right input.** Don't make guesses about how things are. If you don't know, ask someone who does. Different aspects of a plan should be contributed by those most familiar and knowledgeable with these features.

- **Planning requires thought about what else might happen.** Your plan is unlikely to develop activities in isolation. Possible side effects, particularly on other parts of the business need to be considered and taken into account in final proposals.

- **Planning should have some degree of flexibility.** It is not always possible for plans to have one hundred per cent accuracy. There will always be external or internal factors which enforce changes, and it is important that plans include some element of flexibility to permit amendments necessary to maintain progress to an intended goal in the event of significant changes in circumstances

- **Plans should be realistic.** It is little use making plans that are too ambitious and become impossible to carry out. On the other hand, they should not be so timid in their intentions that that fail to achieve a valid purpose.

- **Plans must adequately communicated**. You increase the chances of your plan being successful if the people intended to carry it out are well informed. Conversely, if they are not well informed, you increase the chances of something going wrong.

Strategic and operational planning

- **Strategic planning**. Strategic planning will involve all of the organisation's activities, will in particular be concerned with overall financial resources and budgets, with broad principles of organisation, determining responsibilities for the main functions, and setting key objectives and achievement dates. The time scale of strategic planning can extend from several months to several years. Strategic planning will usually be carried out by senior management and may not form part of your executive responsibilities, but it is important that you appreciate its purpose. Nothing happens in business without strategic planning. It not only sets the overall purpose and direction of business activities, but determines policies, describes the parameters within which individual functions are required to perform, establishes the characteristics of operational management responsibilities, and provides a structure for guiding, as well as harnessing the results of, localised project management.

- **Operational planning**. These are the plans developed by the individual units within an organisation to give effect to its strategic plan. They will define the actions needed to maintain operational effectiveness including the use of resources, co-ordinating with other units, setting individual assignments of work, scheduling and supervising performance, providing instruction and training, and maintaining day-to-day work controls. Many of the circumstances involved will make the time factor a relatively short one, covering anything from one day, to one week, to one month, but in some situations, where more complex projects are involved, a longer period may be required. It is this area of planning with which you are likely to be involved, and the following section sets out an appropriate framework for developing an operational plan.

Constructing an operational plan

Whatever the scale of the project, obtaining answers in each of the following stages will enable you to construct an effective plan for its implementation.

● **Outline the project:**
What is its purpose?
What are its objectives?
When is the start date?
When is the end date?

 I already do this [ ]   I need to revise my approach [ ]

● **Define the activities:**
What tasks have to be undertaken?
How are activities to be allocated?
Are there different stages requiring different activities or allocations?
Will you need to reassign or reschedule current task activity?

 I already do this [ ]   I need to revise my approach [ ]

● **Check available resources:**
What do you have in terms of:
• staffing?
• equipment?
• materials, including documentation?

 I already do this [ ]   I need to revise my approach [ ]

● **Estimate additional resource requirements**
What else do you need in terms of:

• staffing?
• equipment?
• materials, including documentation?

Do you need to consider different requirements for different stages?

Will you need to arrange staff training?

 I already do this [ ]   **I need to revise my approach** [ ]

● **Calculate the cost**

What additional cost will be required for:
• staffing?
• equipment?
• materials?
• training?

Will the total cost be covered by your existing budget, or do you need to negotiate more?

 I already do this [ ]   **I need to revise my approach** [ ]

● **Finalise your proposal**

Review, fine-tune, and confirm the detail from each stage of planning.

Set down your complete proposal in its finalised form.

It may be advisable to draw up a project calendar (See below).

 I already do this [ ]   **I need to revise my approach** [ ]

● **Communicate your intention**

Choose which method(s) of communication you will use to ensure:
• the project team are well briefed.
• others who need to know are informed.

(See *Improving your communication* in Module #4)

☑ **I already do this [ ]   I need to revise my approach [ ]**

Preparing a project calendar

A project calendar which can be shown to the people involved, will make it easier to communicate what you want them to do, and easier for you to keep track of progress.

In its simplest form, a project calendar should describe:

- a layout of days, weeks, or months appropriate to the time required
- a date for the start of the project
- a date for the end of the project.

Using a coloured highlight or marking pen to draw a line joining the two dates will provide a visual record of the number of weeks or months allocated to the project and make it easier to track progress. You may, of course, use a computer to lay out the calendar.

Where a project has been broken down into separate stages, the project calendar should show the timing for each stage.

The project calendar could additionally show a **set of control points -** milestones which show how much work should be completed by a certain date, and by which progress towards the objective can be measured.

This could be by some form of unit count such as units of production, units of monetary value, number or value of sales, number of documents processed, etc.

There are many different varieties of project calendars available. Use one that suits your particular requirements. The Project Calendar shown below is an example of a simple version you can draw up for yourself. It shows:

- a project of four stages extending over 24 weeks
- highlighted control points (unit counts) in weeks 8, 12, 16, 20, 24
- progress update distribution in weeks 9,13,17, 21
- preparation of the project end report in week 25
- and distribution of the end report in week 26

Project stage	1	2	3	4	5	6	7	8	9	10	11	12	13	14	15	16	17	18	19	20	21	22	23	24	25	26
Stage 1	▓	▓	▓	▓																						
Stage 2						▓	▓	▓	▓																	
Stage 3																▓	▓		▓	▓			▓	▓		
Stage 4																			▓	▓			▓	▓	▓	
Unit count						▯				▯				▯				▯				▯				
Distribute updates								▯				▯				▯				▯						
Prepare end report																									▯	
Distribute end report																										▯

Developing your planning skill

The following steps will help you ensure that your plans are practical, well-supported, and can be successfully carried out.

- **Make time for planning.** Planning is part of a manager's job. Make time for it in the same way as for other aspects of your work. Careful planning may take time, but it is never time wasted. Nor is it necessarily time-consuming, and it has been repeatedly demonstrated that time spent planning can be more than made up through speedy and successful implementation.

 I already do this [ ]   I need to revise my approach [ ]

- **Make planning a routine.** All task activities will benefit from planning. Prepare plans as matter of routine and encourage subordinates to do the same. Keep the format and style of plan simple. Avoid paper mountains.

 I already do this [ ]   I need to revise my approach [ ]

- **Involve your boss.** Discuss objectives, goals, and outline proposals with your superior. This will help you ensure that your

85

plans are consistent with the organisation's overall business plan, and are consistent with established objectives, practices, and policies. You are also likely to obtain a valuable, different perspective to your line of thinking, and having your boss's support will make it easier to obtain additional resources.

 I already do this [ ]   I need to revise my approach [ ]

- **Involve subordinates**. If the activities involve subordinates, so should the planning. They may contribute valuable input about methods, resources, problems, and their involvement will result in a higher level of commitment to the arrangements made.

 I already do this [ ]   I need to revise my approach [ ]

- **Involve everyone else who will be affected**. Unless the plan is a very secret one, include those responsible for implementation, those who will benefit, those who will supply resources, other affected departments or customers. Let them know your intention as early as possible in case they can provide feedback that needs to be taken into account in your arrangements.

 I already do this [ ]   I need to revise my approach [ ]

- **Make sure the resources you need are available**. Plans without the necessary budget, equipment, supplies, or people to make them work are no more than pipe dreams.

 I already do this [ ]   I need to revise my approach [ ]

- **Review plans regularly**. Keep abreast of progress, modify arrangements to meet changing circumstances, and keep a schedule visible so that everyone involved can also keep informed and abreast of progress.

 I already do this [ ]   I need to revise my approach [ ]

Managing a project

This is the second principal area of project management. It follows directly on from the planning stage. It is concerned with keeping the project organised and progressing, with tracking progress, monitoring resources and costs, maintaining distribution of relevant updated information, and deciding on appropriate responses to any problems that arise.

In order to do these things, you will need to ensure you have appropriate systems in place to keep yourself informed and in control.

Setting up controls and monitor systems

The section on Controls in Module #2 discusses the general purpose and procedures for setting up controls as a means of monitoring employee performance and development. Which method of control is used, will depend on the activity involved, but it is essential that it should be able to monitor ongoing results and provide ongoing comparisons in sufficiently measurable terms to allow decisions to be taken about appropriate actions to manage project activities and keep performance in line with expectations. It will therefore be necessary to check if existing control systems will adequately cover project requirements, or if amendments will be needed, or if new systems will need to be devised and introduced.

 I already do this [ ]   I need to revise my approach [ ]

In the specific case of project management controls, the same general setting up procedures apply, but the focus is more on obtaining information about the progress of task activities and other aspects of the project operation. Applying periodic checks at critical stages or set intervals of the project's development (control points) will enable you to do this, will enable you to respond appropriately to any new developments or changes in circumstances in order to keep the project on course, and will enable you to build up a reference record of progress.

 I already do this [ ]   I need to revise my approach [ ]

Updating information

While it is important for you to keep informed about the progress of task activities and other aspects of the project operation, it is also important that the others involved are kept up to date with what is happening. Regular updates of progress will help to maintain their involvement and their commitment; information about new developments or changes in circumstance may enable them to adjust their actions to better effect, and to feedback any relevant information that could assist your overall control.

 I already do this [ ]   I need to revise my approach [ ]

Dealing with problems

This is very much part of a manager's responsibilities. Careful preparation at the planning stage may anticipate and remove some potential difficulties, but in project management, which generally involves the development of new activities or using existing activities in new situations, there is always the possibility that problems will arise at some stage of the project.

When they do, it is neither sensible to assume they will have no effect on the project outcome, nor is it permissible to allow them to remain without response. Left to themselves, problems seldom go away. They can easily attach themselves to project activities, becoming adopted as part of them. Where this happens, they can disrupt planned procedures, restrict the effectiveness of work processes, and lessen the outcome of the project. It will be up to you to ensure this does not happen.

The first step in dealing with any problem is simply to acknowledge that it is there. Fortunately for all of us, problems do not keep to themselves. Like an unexpected gatecrasher intent on spoiling a party, they will be unwelcome, and may not tells us how they have arrived, but will make their presence known quite quickly, sometimes even spectacularly, and will grab as much of the action as they can. If you have met that kind of situation at a party, you will know there is no point in pretending the gatecrasher is not there, and hoping he will go away. If you do, things will go from bad to worse. Yet, when faced with an unexpected and unwelcome problem at work, this is exactly how some managers respond. Things, of course, go from bad to worse.

To deal with the gatecrasher, you would acknowledge he is there, single him out, and take steps to stop his disruptive behaviour spoiling your party. You would get rid of him as soon as you could, and make sure he didn't come back. You might need help to do it, but that's what you would do.

It is also what you should do with a problem.

Don't leave things to go from bad to worse. Acknowledge it is there, isolate it, find out what caused it, and take action to stop it disrupting your processes and procedures, and derailing the outcome of your project. Get rid of it as soon as you can, and make sure it doesn't come back. You might need help to do it, but that's what you should do.

 I already do this [ ]   I need to revise my approach [ ]

Recognising a problem

Problems are often unexpected, but are not usually difficult to spot. Disruptions to processes and procedures, or a falling off in the level of performance or the quality of work, or signs of discontent among staff, or a pattern of complaints from clients or customers are usually easily identified indications that there is some problem that needs to be dealt with.

If there is evidence of this kind, even if you are not sure what the problem might be or where it may lie, it makes no sense to ignore that there might be something wrong. All that does is to delay the inevitable, and things might be much more difficult to sort out when you do eventually get round to it. It makes much better sense to find out if there is a problem, and to set about putting things right as soon as you can.

 I already do this [ ]   I need to revise my approach [ ]

Responding to a problem

If you know there is a problem, or even suspect there is one, put it to the top of your list of priorities. Whatever else you do, you should make it your urgent business to enquire into the circumstances that lead you to believe there is something wrong somewhere.

 I already do this [ ]   I need to revise my approach [ ]

Questions you can set yourself to answer include:

● **What evidence of a problem is there, and where does it lie?** If there is a problem, the signs will be there. If your operational controls are working as they should, it will not be difficult to tell if any of the activities is failing to meet your expectations. With this knowledge, you will be able to tell if there really is a problem, and to see where it lies. If you find it difficult to tell exactly what the problem is or where it lies, but are still concerned there is something wrong, the problem, or part of it, may have to do with the controls which are either giving you wrong information or not enough, and you may need to refine these.

● **What is the cause?** Having identified where the problem lies, it should be a relatively easy matter to compare what is being done with what should be done to isolate the cause. However, since problem causes can arise in any area of your operation's activity or in any combination of them, you may need to check out more than one of them to get to the real reason why thing are going wrong. You may not only need to establish where, but also to find out who, what, why, when, and how?

● **What are the facts?** Are they to do with:
  • **Staff**: skills, training. deployment, numbers, supervision, working conditions, work levels, morale, communication?
  • **Equipment**: quality, quantity, capability, outdated, poorly programmed, badly maintained?
  • **Materials**: quality, quantity, availability, design?

- **Procedures**: inadequate, inappropriate; haphazard, outdated?
- **Controls**: restrictive, incomplete, ineffectual, lapsed?
- ... or what?

Only consider evidence that can be verified. Try to link verified evidence back to affected performance. Links that can be established should point to the real causes, and should indicate where the solution lies.

- **Does it need a quick response, or is there time to plan and prepare?** The answer to that will depend on how serious the problem is. As a general rule of thumb, the more serious the problem is, the more urgently it needs to be dealt with. You will need to make a judgement about that. But the demands of business are not always consistent with the time available to deal with them, and if you need to buy time for a more considered arrangement to be put in place, a quick temporary or partial fix that allows for some remedial action is better than no response at all.

- **Is it a problem I can deal with, or do I need to refer it on?** Your answer to this question will depend partly on how serious the problem is, partly on what needs to be done to put things right, partly on whether it falls within the limits of action you are able to take, and partly on how confident you are about your ability to do what is required. If it is within the limits of your authority and you can handle it, go ahead. If it is a matter you need to refer on, don't just report it. Refer it on with a summary of the problem, its location, its cause(s), your assessment of the urgency of the situation, any temporary or partial action you have taken to address the issue, and any suggestions for further remedial action you think should be considered.

Solving a problem

Knowing you have a problem is one thing; solving it is quite another. Nevertheless, it is almost inevitable that project management will involve problem solving, both before and during the project's operation, and you will need to do it. The processes involved in problem solving are very closely related to those required in decision making, which is covered in Module #4, but it will be more helpful to your management of projects to regard problem solving as a separate and distinct activity.

While decision making is concerned with judgements and choosing between different possible course of action, problem solving is usually concerned with factually determining the nature and cause of some deviation or gap between actual and expected performance, and the actions required to correct the situation.

The first step in problem solving is to understand the type of problem to be dealt with.

There are two main types of problems, and they require different forms of problem solving.

- **Programmed problems**. These are the routine problems which managers face on a day-to-day basis. Examples include equipment breakdown, defective materials, delayed supplies, staff absences and so on. They may sometimes be difficult, but solutions can be usually found by following precedent, procedures, systems, or company practice. Computers can help where there is a complex numerical content, and there are different methods, such as decision tree techniques, which can be used with programmed problems. In general, programmed problems are routine, can if necessary be anticipated and prepared for in advance, and have a single correct solution.

- **Non-programmed problems**. These are problems which managers are faced with from time to time, and for which there is no precedent, or system, or procedure for determining the right course of action. Examples include problems which are being tackled for the first time, problems which no longer respond effectively to previous remedies, developing a new procedure, or a new product, or a new marketing campaign, or simply managing a crisis. Non-programmed problems require a unique, creative solution to be found. It may be possible for the manager to develop an original, personal response, or it may be appropriate to involve others. Group problem solving such as by brainstorming sessions is frequently used and can be very effective.

Generating solutions

It is unlikely that you will need to generate creative solutions for programmed problems. The response to them will be found by following precedent, procedures, systems, or company practice, and will only need action to reinforce or re-establish the appropriate process to bring the situation into line.

It is, however, more than likely that you will need to generate creative solutions where non-programmed problems are concerned. By their nature, neither non-programmed problems nor their solutions are likely to follow precedent. Nor are they likely to be contained in established procedures, systems, or company practices. You will therefore need to set these preconditions aside, and to separate idea generation from compliance with what is usually required, accepted and adhered to in task activity.

In your search for a creative solution, you may find it helpful to involve others, particularly those whose work activities are linked in some way to the area in which the problem lies. Involving others will not only increase the number who can contribute possible solutions, it will also increase your sources of information. Even if some of what you learn is conflicting, it will extend your understanding of the real issues and make it more certain that you are responding to the problem and not just the symptoms.

Two frequently and easily used methods of creative problem solving which involve others, are brainstorming, and nominal group technique. Both methods require you to make some work-free time to get people together. It may seem counter-productive to take people away from their normal work to try to deal with a problem, but half an hour of concentrated group effort may be the only way to get to the root of the problem and may save days of disruption and several hours of remedial work later on.

- **Brainstorming**. The objective is to generate as many problem solving ideas as possible. Quantity not quality is required
  - **Include all people involved in the area of work** in which the problem has arisen, and make it clear that they are free to propose ideas, however extreme, without fear of criticism or censure.
  - **Start by stating the problem**, and if necessary explain how brainstorming works - in simple terms, you think, I record, we evaluate.
  - **Lead into the session** using an 'In how many ways …?' format. For example, 'In how many ways does [the problem] affect our operation?' or 'In how many way could we stop [the problem] from happening.' or 'In how many ways could we change things to reduce [the problem]?', and so on. If necessary use questions like these in succession to stimulate the flow of ideas.
  - **Encourage any ideas to come forward**, however wild or offbeat.
  - **Record all ideas** on a flipchart, and keep these in view throughout the session to encourage participants to build on each other's ideas.
  - **Energise the group** by setting goals, such as 'Only 5 more ideas to reach 20 or 30 or 40' and so on.
  - **If ideas begin to dry up**, ask more 'In how many ways.....' questions.
  - **If you are sure there are no more ideas** forthcoming, stop this part of the session. Do not allow it to drag on and drift into other matters.
  - **Declare a short break**, tea or coffee if appropriate, and use this time to **group recorded ideas** into manageable categories, and decide criteria (practicality, time, cost, etc.) for evaluating each category.
  - **Reconvene**, discuss each category, aim to select the three or four best ideas in each category, discard unworkable ideas and record the remainder for further, more detailed consideration.

- **Nominal group technique**. This is a modification of brainstorming which involves only a selected group of participants. As far as possible, take one from each area of work included in the project. It can be the best method if there is difficulty making a work free time for everyone involved.

- **Membership is restricted**, usually to those most directly involved, and usually a small percentage of the total, for example, 6 from a group of 20.
- **Start by stating the problem**, and if necessary explain how the nominal group technique works; in simple terms - we think, we record, we evaluate.
- **Lead into the session** using the 'In how many ways.......?' format. For example, 'In how many ways does [the problem] affect our operation?' or 'In how many way could we stop [the problem] from happening.' or 'In how many ways could we change things to reduce [the problem]?', and so on. If necessary use questions like these in succession to stimulate the flow of ideas.
- **Ask members to write down** their ideas, instead of stating them verbally.
- **When you are sure there are no more ideas forthcoming** from one 'How many ways' question, introduce another one. When there are no more questions to put to the group, stop this part of the session.
- **Ask members to read out their ideas** one at a time. Work on a round robin basis and record each idea on a flipchart in a few words. Continue until all ideas are recorded.
- **Discuss ideas in turn** for clarification and evaluation.
- **Select the best ideas** by secret independent voting, and record these for further, more detailed consideration.

Whichever method is chosen

- **Go for quantity.** Generate as many ideas as possible. Problems are sometimes solved by combining a number of ideas.
- **Suspend judgement.** Don't make or allow any criticism or evaluation of ideas until as many as possible have been generated.
- **Keep it open.** Encourage all sorts of ideas. Even far-fetched

and silly ideas can lead on to something more realistic .
* **Cross-fertilise**. Encourage members to build on each other's ideas.

Choosing a solution

The participation of others will help to gain their commitment and support for the action that needs to be taken, but the final choice of a solution will remain your responsibility. Having followed the processes outlined above, you should now have a short-list of the best ideas, and should be well on the way to making your final choice a carefully considered one.

To gain a realistic evaluation of its likely success before committing yourself, your reputation, and whatever resources of money, people and materials will be involved, consider these three points:

● Will the solution work?
● Will it fix the problem?
● Will it prevent the problem from recurring?

You won't really know the answers to these questions until you start to put your solution into effect, but by checking out how well it is likely to do the following things before you introduce it, you will get a good indication of what the outcome is likely to be. In doing so, you also give yourself the opportunity to make a final comparison between your short-listed solutions, and increase your chances of making the best choice.

For the solution to work it, will need to be:

● practical and able to be applied within the project
● acceptable to those who will use it or will be affected by it
● ethical, legal, and compliant with statutory requirements such as Health & Safety regulations.

For it to fix the problem, it will need to be:

● able to correct or replace faulty elements in the original process
● able to retain any beneficial elements of the original process
● able to achieve required objectives and standards of performance.

For it to prevent the problem from recurring, it will need to be:
- able to work within the project
- robustly integrated with other project processes
- monitored, and if necessary adjusted, during early stages.

If you can satisfy yourself on those points, your will have a solution that is workable, will fix the problem, will stop it from happening again, and will enable you to continue towards the successful conclusion of your project.

You may still have to convince your boss or other member of senior management that your proposed solution is justified, particularly if it involves additional costs, say for people or equipment. If you have followed the guidance given on the preceding pages, you will be able to show that your solution is practical and defensible. If you also show that without the action you propose, the problem will remain, will continue to adversely affect results, and is more likely to worsen than get better, you are likely to get full approval to go ahead.

Concluding a project

This is the third principal area of project management, and is its key learning zone. It is concerned with calculating the end result, evaluating performance, analysing what went right or wrong, and assembling these together to produce an end of project report. It is an appropriate point for those involved in the project to get together to discuss the operation and express their views on what went right or wrong. It also gives the manager an opportunity to review the overall effectiveness of his project management, and consider where improvements could be made. Lessons learned at this stage can have a significant effect on day to day work schedules as well as on future projects.

Calculating end results
This should not just be about comparing two sets of figures - final achievement versus required achievement, but should also include calculations of final costs versus budget, and may need to include items such as total materials usage versus materials estimates, total materials wastage versus materials costs, actual staffing versus expected staffing, and actual time versus expected time.

 I already do this [ ]   **I need to revise my approach** [ ]

Evaluating performance
As well as considering how well people have performed in project activities, your evaluation should also look at the reasonableness of objectives, how well the systems and procedures set up for the project have worked, the suitability and reliability of equipment, and to what extent each of these has assisted or impeded project operations.

 I already do this [ ]   **I need to revise my approach** [ ]

What went right or wrong
Your analysis of what went right or wrong should try to answer why

things happened as they did; what made things better or worse? what caused them to happen? what has been done or can be done to lock in the good things, shut out the bad ones, and avoid recurrence of any problems encountered?

 I already do this [ ]   I need to revise my approach [ ]

Producing and distributing an end of project report

You may or may not be required to prepare an end of project report, but even if you are not asked to do so, there is much to be gained from compiling an account of how things have gone and what has been achieved. Setting them down on paper is a good way to check that all aspects of the project have been properly concluded, and there are no loose ends. It will give you a record of what has been done and what has been learned that can be referred to on other occasions and may contribute usefully to the development of your management skills. It is also the best way to provide appropriate information to those who need to know,

The guidance notes given earlier in this Module will help you prepare and present a project report.

 I already do this [ ]   I need to revise my approach [ ]

Reviewing the overall effectiveness of your project management

There are sensible questions you can put to yourself, and valuable lessons you can learn from the answers. Did you achieve your key objectives? How good was your contribution? Did things work out as you intended? Was your planning adequate, sufficiently detailed, and sufficiently focused on the project's requirements? Was it well enough communicated to those who needed to know? What about your controls and monitor systems - did they enable you to keep things properly progressing? Did you keep those involved regularly updated about progress? How well did you deal with any problems?

☑ **I already do this [ ]   I need to revise my approach [ ]**

Having asked these questions, consider if there are things you would do differently to improve a similar situation. If there are, write them down and keep them as a personal guideline for future use.

Personal Progress Review
Module #3

Start date of Module #3: _____
1st review date:_____ 2nd review date:_____

If you have followed the guidance given in the preceding pages, you should have made valuable progress in developing your management knowledge and skills. To evaluate your progress, you should now complete the following section by marking an assessment on each of the rating scales to show the extent of change evident since the start of this module.

Please remember that this programme is designed to help you develop your management knowledge and skills through self-managed active learning. It is you who will make it work, and you who will benefit. The circumstances of your appointment may not make the same degree of progress possible in every area of activity, and in some you may not, at this stage, have made as much progress as you like. If this is the case, don't mislead yourself by marking above your achievement. Build on what you have done, and try again. You will gain most advantage from your efforts by making your assessment as honestly and realistically as you can.

Planning a project

On a scale of 1 - 10, where 5 represents (a) your estimate of the effectiveness of your previous planning technique and (b) your estimate of your previous planning skill, indicate to what extent you consider these to have improved or worsened as a result of action you have taken, or knowledge you have gained from this module.

Worsened   Previously   Improved
After 1 month: [1] [2] [3] [4] [5] [6] [7] [8] [9] [10]
After 2 months: [1] [2] [3] [4] [5] [6] [7] [8] [9] [10]

101

Managing a project

On a scale of 1 - 10, where 5 represents your estimate of the effectiveness of your ability to keep project activities organised and progressing, indicate to what extent you consider this to have been improved or worsened as a result of action you have taken, or knowledge you have gained, from this module.

Worsened   Previously   Improved
After 1 month: [1] [2] [3] [4] [5] [6] [7] [8] [9] [10]
After 2 months: [1] [2] [3] [4] [5] [6] [7] [8] [9] [10]

On a scale of 1 - 10, where 5 represents your estimate of the effectiveness of previous controls and monitor systems, indicate to what extent you consider these to have been improved or worsened as a result of action you have taken, or knowledge you have gained, from this module.

Worsened   Previously   Improved
After 1 month: [1] [2] [3] [4] [5] [6] [7] [8] [9] [10]
After 2 months: [1] [2] [3] [4] [5] [6] [7] [8] [9] [10]

On a scale of 1 - 10, where 5 represents your estimate of how effectively you dealt with problems previously, indicate to what extent you consider your problem solving ability to have improved or worsened as a result of action you have taken, or knowledge you have gained, from this module.

Worsened   Previously   Improved
After 1 month: [1] [2] [3] [4] [5] [6] [7] [8] [9] [10]
After 2 months: [1] [2] [3] [4] [5] [6] [7] [8] [9] [10]

Concluding a project

On scale of 1 - 10, where 5 represents your estimate of your previous ability make an effective project conclusion, indicate to what extent you consider your effectiveness to have been increased or decreased as a result of action you have taken, or knowledge you have gained, from this module.

Decrease   Previously   Increase

After 1 month: [1] [2] [3] [4] [5] [6] [7] [8] [9] [10]

After 2 months: [1] [2] [3] [4] [5] [6] [7] [8] [9] [10]

END OF MODULE #3

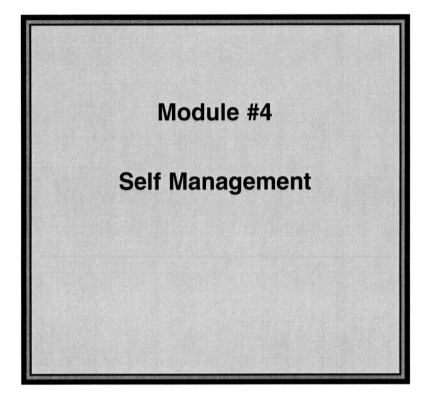

Module #4

Self Management

Start date for this module _____

The challenges facing managers are more complex, and more pressurised by the demands of meeting performance standards and production deadlines, than at any previous time. It therefore makes good sense to ensure that the core of your management operation - your management of yourself - makes sufficient use of well-established processes for you to meet and respond to the requirements of your appointment with better assurance of success.

Managing your time

Time is the most critical resource you have. Since it is strictly limited, can be used only once, cannot be saved or accumulated, and any that is wasted cannot be regained, its effective use is an essential management skill.

A typical workday for most managers may involve responding to mail, originating correspondence, preparing reports, discussing projects with colleagues or subordinates, constructing and issuing instructions, making and receiving phone calls, attending meetings, and interacting with others who make unscheduled contact to talk through some aspect of business. It may also involve other things, such as business travel, and it may frequently seem that there just aren't enough hours to get everything done.

Recent research has found that in some cases, as much as 50% of a manager's time can be wasted on activities which do not achieve meaningful results, and that even managers who consider themselves good at 'getting things done' may be losing as much as 30% of their own productive effectiveness by having no personal programme of time management.

Successful time management has three aspects.

- It means choosing and using a time management system and sticking to it.
- It means focusing attention on the key results activities of your appointment
- It involves the elimination of the time robbers which are common to every management activity.

Choosing and using a time management system

Develop your own personal time management system. There is no one best way. Choose one that meets your needs, suits your way of doing things, and is easy to use. Essentially, it should enable you to plan and programme your activities. It needs to be date specific. The simplest form is a diary, but there are other options such as an electronic organiser, or a weekly, monthly, or annual wall chart, or you may find it helpful to use a combination of these. Whatever you choose, stick to it. Success comes from using your system in a consistent and disciplined way.

☑   **I already do this [ ]   I need to revise my approach [ ]**

By keeping track of what you are doing and what you are committed to on future dates, you will be better able to ensure that -

- you don't become overloaded
- you can co-ordinate with others
- you can adjust better to urgent new requirements
- you can maintain focus on key results activities.

There are many commercial versions available, and most PC word-processing software includes some form of time management paperwork which can be customised to meet your requirements. An example of an easy to use daily task sheet which can significantly support your time management is given at the end of this section.

Focusing attention on key results activities

Key results activities are those that are essential to achieving required performance objectives as opposed to those that are concerned with maintenance (procedures) or research or reporting.

It is certain that you won't get 10 hours of activity into 8. Something will have to go and you can choose what that something is.

- You can drop things off the end of the table and ignore them.
- You can put things aside and hope to catch up with them later.
- You can eat into your own time - the time you need to refresh yourself, to be with your family and manage your personal commitments. (You may need to put in extra time and effort on certain occasions, but to do it as an ongoing arrangement is not a good idea.).

- Or you can look at things in a different way and begin to manage your situation by focusing on the key results activities of your appointment through task selection.

Conducting task selection

- **Distinguish between urgent and important tasks**. Even though a task is urgent, it may not have an important bearing on key results, and you should try to get it out of the way as quickly as possible. Tasks which affect key results are important and should be given the time they deserve.

☑ **I already do this** [ ]   **I need to revise my approach** [ ]

- **Eliminate unnecessary tasks.** List all the tasks you do in one complete cycle of the department's activities (this may be weekly or monthly), and consider their value. Start with those that have been put 'on the back burner'. If they have been there for more than one complete cycle, they are probably unnecessary and should be considered for deletion from your task list

  Next, select the least important tasks, up to 25% of your list. Consider if they really do need to be done by checking the cost in time or expenditure against the benefits obtained. Tasks that take a great deal of time, but make little contribution to key results are probably unnecessary and should be considered for deletion from your task list.

  Alternately, some of these tasks may be ripe for delegation. (See *Delegation*, Module #2)

  The choice is sometimes difficult, and you may need to consult with a colleague or your boss, but you should aim to weed out unnecessary tasks and give yourself more time to concentrate on those that are essential to achieving key results.

☑ **I already do this** [ ]   **I need to revise my approach** [ ]

- **Prioritise. Prioritise. Prioritise.** Check out each remaining entry in your task list, and give it a priority rating. Obviously tasks with approaching deadlines, tasks that seriously affect others, tasks that would result in dire consequences if ignored, and tasks that impinge on your credibility are likely to be high priorities. These are the things you must get done that day. Using the daily task sheet at the end of this section, these items would be listed at the top and coded 'A'.

  Next, list the tasks of medium importance, those that should be completed during the day, but will not cause major problems if carried over. Using the daily task sheet, these items would be coded 'B'.

  Finally list the remainder, items that are important enough to do, but not immediately. Using the daily task sheet, these items would be coded 'C'

☑ **I already do this [ ]   I need to revise my approach [ ]**

Three points to note

- Priorities change from day to day as the department's work cycle progresses. Therefore, each day requires a new daily task sheet. Fixing each new sheet on top of the previous day's sheet to form a 'pad'(run a Pritt stick along the top front edge of the old sheet and press the top back edge of the new one on to it to hold them together) will give you a record of progress on prioritised tasks over any period you choose. It will also make it easier to keep track of tasks that have been carried over from one day to the next.

- You may find that preparing your daily task sheet in advance, i.e. at the end of the previous day, will get you off to a better start for dealing with its priorities.

- Try to deal with 'A' coded items at a time of the day when you are likely to be most mentally alert. Some people are mentally sluggish first thing in the morning, and may need a half hour or so to reach their peak efficiency time. If this is you, try dealing with a 'B' or 'C' item first, alternately intersperse an occasional 'B' or 'C' item as a mental break from top priority projects during the day.

Eliminating time robbers

There are numerous traps that managers can fall into when trying to make effective use of their time. These will rob you of the time needed to deal with key results activities.

- The worst time robber is not to devote the greatest amount of your time to your key results activities, and lack of attention to planning and organising, and failing to prioritise are common and usually fairly evident contributors. These things can, however, be easily identified, and can be corrected by the sensible and consistent use of task selection as described above. Some other common time robbers are set down below, together with suggestions for dealing with them.

- **Telephone calls.** Some will be essential, but when they occur during your most productive times they break your concentration and disrupt your train of thought. Try to give yourself a 'call free zone' by persuading people to call you between set times. Delegate routine enquiries and arrange a call back system for returning calls at a low priority time of your day.

 I already do this [ ]   I need to revise my approach [ ]

- **The uninvited visitor.** When this person walks into your office, get up and go to meet him or her. Be polite and respond to quickly answerable questions. Do not offer a seat or sit down yourself. Explain that you are busy on an important task, and arrange a more suitable time for longer discussion.

 I already do this [ ]   I need to revise my approach [ ]

- **Paperwork**. Develop a system for handling each piece of paper once only. Decide what to do with each piece of paper as it comes on to your desk. Then get rid of it. Whether you pass it on, file it, sign it, revise it, return it, redirect it, or throw it away, the key is to take action right away. File regularly.

  ☑ **I already do this** [ ] **I need to revise my approach** [ ]

- **Over-commitment**. Being eager to please can result in becoming over-burdened. Don't agree to take on everything you are asked to do without first asking, 'Is it really important?' 'Will it help me achieve my goals?' 'Can someone else do it?' Learn to say, 'No.'

  ☑ **I already do this** [ ] **I need to revise my approach** [ ]

- **Travel and waiting**. If you have to go somewhere, build the time into your schedule of Things To Do. Long journeys by train, for example, are a good opportunity to catch up on paperwork or necessary information about products, services, systems, etc.

  ☑ **I already do this** [ ] **I need to revise my approach** [ ]

- **Meetings**. Attend essential meetings only. Delegate attendance to others where it is practical to do so. When you hold meetings, prepare in advance, insist that others are prepared as well, and keep to a strict schedule.

  ☑ **I already do this** [ ] **I need to revise my approach** [ ]

- **Lack of energy**. Personal energy levels rise and fall throughout the day and week. Find out how your energy levels rise and fall. Schedule demanding tasks for your high energy times, and deal with more routine matters during low energy times.

   I already do this [ ] I need to **revise my approach** [ ]

- **Poor health and lack of fitness**. A massive time robber. Keep yourself in shape with physically and mentally stimulating activities outside of work. Eat a moderate and varied diet. Build in sufficient time for all aspects of your life, family, friends, and other interests.

☑ I already do this [ ] I need to revise my approach [ ]

- **Procrastination**. Frequently the result of poor planning and a failure to prioritise, procrastination is the classic time robber. Putting things off because they are unpleasant, or difficult, will not make them any more pleasant or any less difficult when you are forced to do them. The more you delay, the more you build up your resistance to the task, the more you will put yourself under pressure to complete to a deadline. The rush to complete procrastinated tasks at the last minute inevitably means that some deadlines will be missed and some quality will be sacrificed. Try breaking unpleasant or difficult tasks down into more easily handled parts, and make a start. Once you begin to make progress, the rest will follow more easily.

☑ I already do this [ ] I need to revise my approach [ ]

Think also about delegating part or parts, or simply asking someone for help.

Daily task sheet: example

THINGS TO DO TODAY   **Date** _____

Priority   Done
code

[ ] 1 _____ [ ]

[ ] 2 _____ [ ]

[ ] 3 _____ [ ]

[ ] 4 _____ [ ]

[ ] 5 _____ [ ]

[ ] 6 _____ [ ]

[ ] 7 _____ [ ]

[ ] 8 _____ [ ]

[ ] 9 _____ [ ]

[ ] 10 _____ [ ]

[ ] 11 _____ [ ]

[ ] 12 _____ [ ]

[ ] 13 _____ [ ]

[ ] 14 _____ [ ]

[ ] 15 _____ [ ]

Notes

Making your decisions

Business decisions are always important. They can be crucial to business success, and can be enormously influential. They require knowledge, judgement, a good sense of purpose, and may also demand courage. They are seldom easy to make or take, but are an essential part of any management appointment.

Decision making is essentially about deliberately choosing between two or more options for action. In making that choice, which may include the option to take no action, the process will also involve evaluating the risks and consequences that each option presents. Any decision that ignores these evaluations is unlikely to properly resolve the issues involved, and may introduce a worsening situation.

In some areas of business, decision making is becoming increasingly systemised. With developing technology, computers can have the parameters of option risks, consequences, and other conditions built into their programs. Given relevant information, they will evaluate it against the set parameters and will produce a systemised decision. Decision making of this kind is arrived at by processing information, and in some situations will be all that is needed for decision-based action to be taken.

However, there are limits to how much the computer can do, and to how much access to computer-based decisions there is for managers faced with having to make decisions across a range of day to day matters about local business operating conditions. In most cases it will still be for the manager to judge when and on which matters decisions need to be made, and when and how the action should be implemented. Even with the support of computer technology, there is always likely to be a place for human assessment, and there is always likely to be a need for managers to make and take certain decisions, and to develop decision-making as a personal skill.

Faced with a situation that needs to be resolved, there is a logical sequence you can follow that will enable you to make a well considered decision. Keeping to the sequence whenever you are faced with having to make a decision will help you develop your decision making skill.

113

To begin the process, you will need to ask yourself the following questions:

'Why am I making this decision? Do I really understand the circumstances, and the restraints or opportunities that make the decision necessary?' If not, you cannot safely proceed further until you are satisfied that you do.

 I already do this [ ]   I need to revise my approach [ ]

'What are the components of each circumstance? Do I have enough information to make a valid analysis of the issues involved?' If not, you cannot safely proceed further until you are satisfied that you do.

 I already do this [ ]   I need to revise my approach [ ]

'Which of those issues should the decision address? Can I clearly identify the situation that now requires the decision?' If not, you cannot safely proceed further until you are satisfied that you can.

 I already do this [ ]   I need to revise my approach [ ]

'What options for action are open to me? Have I explored and identified all the possibilities for action available to me, and where necessary have sought help from those best placed to advise?' If not, you cannot safely proceed further until you are satisfied that you have.

 I already do this [ ]   I need to revise my approach [ ]

'Which option will best improve the situation? Do I know enough about the requirements and consequences of each option to select one as an appropriate choice?' If not, you cannot safely proceed further until you are satisfied that you do.

I already do this [ ]   **I need to revise my approach** [ ]

'What are the risks involved? Have I calculated the potential risks and balanced these against the risks of continuing without taking any action to confirm favourable grounds for going ahead?' If not, you cannot safely proceed until you are satisfied that you have.

 I already do this [ ]   I need to **revise my approach** [ ]

'What preparations do I need to make before implementing any change? Have I considered the probable effect on staffing, task allocation, training, equipment, existing procedures, and cost?' If not, you cannot safely proceed further until you are satisfied that you have.

 I already do this [ ]   **I need to revise my approach** [ ]

If you have been able to satisfy yourself on those points, there is still a further question you need to ask yourself.

'What further discussions need to take place? Have I fully informed those who may be affected, and those who need to know?' If not, you cannot safely proceed further until you are satisfied that you have.

 I already do this [ ]   **I need to revise my approach** [ ]

Discussion with those who may be affected and those who need to know is good business sense. Even if you are not immediately aware of it, what you intend to do may have an effect on some other part of the overall business operation within which your activities take place. If you take action without giving those who might be even indirectly affected the opportunity to consider adjustments they may need to make to accommodate any changes to working arrangements arising from your proposed decision, you may invite their opposition, and may prevent your proposal from producing the results you intend. Keeping them informed will avoid this possibility. It will give you the opportunity to obtain any relevant input from them, and to resolve any points of concern they may raise about your proposal. In effect, you will be giving them the opportunity to buy into the proposal and will be more likely to receive their backing for what you intend to do.

If you have satisfied yourself on all of the foregoing points, any potential problems and key issues requiring clarification are likely to have been identified and sorted. You can have better assurance that your decision has been well considered, and will be an effective one, and can now proceed to set up your proposal for action. This should include:

✓ setting a date for action
✓ informing all those involved, affected, and who need to know
✓ undertaking implementation planning (what and how things need to be done)
✓ commencing action
✓ monitoring progress
✓ adjusting as necessary
✓ continuing to monitor progress.

Decision-making will require you to have the following.

● **Knowledge of the operating conditions in which the decision is required.** Restrict your decision-making to those areas of business operation in which you are confident you have sufficient knowledge to determine the criteria on which the decision should be made, and the experience to support and justify your judgement.

☑ I already do this [ ]   I need to revise my approach [ ]

● **Knowledge of the ground rules and limits governing the kinds of decisions you are permitted to take.** No one ever has an entirely free hand in decision-making. The action you can take will be governed by policies and procedures laid down by top management. These are not arbitrary restrictions, but will have been constructed to protect business interests, and to give you the scope you need to get things done without continually referring upwards. Make sure you know the guidelines within which your decisions should be taken, and make full use of the authority you have been given. Remember, it is as a principal function of their appointment that managers are paid to make and take decisions.

 I already do this [ ]   I need to revise my approach [ ]

- **Appreciation of the likely effects of the decision on such matters as revenue, costs, functionality, and morale.** Decisions are seldom, if ever, conducted in isolation or confined exclusively to the situation they are intended to resolve. For example, a decision to purchase new equipment may require changes in Health and Safety Rules, or the re-training or redeployment of personnel, or adjustments to the wage structure to recognise new skills or responsibilities, or it may have a knock-on effect on workload or morale in another part of the business. You therefore not only need to consider each decision for its immediate effect on the matter you wish to resolve, but also for the possible effects it may have on other aspects of your operation, or in other areas of the business.

 I already do this [ ]   I need to revise my approach [ ]

- **A conscious intention to achieve a balanced judgement.** It is not always easy to put aside opinions and prejudices, or to know by how much personal convictions, and moral and ethical values, are influencing judgement. Nevertheless, it is incumbent on all managers that they try to reach decisions that maintain a balance between those values and feelings, and a logical, impartial view of the facts and their practical implications. Questioning the validity of values on the one hand, and the validity of facts on the other, against the essential purpose that the decision is intended to achieve, will give you the opportunity to take better account of the considerations necessary for a balanced judgement.

☑ **I already do this** [　] **I need to revise my approach** [　]

The following are suggested as additional points to consider when making decisions.

- **Decision-making is a skill that can be improved by practice.** Treat each new decision as a step forward rather than a challenge
- **Try to develop effective decisions** that improve performance in key results areas, sound decisions that increase efficiency rather than costs or reduce costs rather than efficiency, and well-considered decisions that enable others to buy into your intention.
- **Avoid getting bogged down in details.** Stick to basics and essentials, and keep focused on the purpose your decision is intended to achieve
- **Seek out all relevant options.** If necessary, talk the situation through with others, and remember even deciding to do nothing can be acceptable if there is no better option.
- **Hold to your decision,** but be prepared to reconsider if circumstances change or new facts come to light
- **Be prepared to defend your decision** and satisfy enquiries by stating your reasons, and defining your purpose, but remember -
- **Decisions change things;** wherever possible give people involved the opportunity to understand and adjust.
- **Prepare the way for decisions that impact on others,** and lessen possible resistance by consulting before forming a conclusion.
- **Don't spend time and energy agonising over minor points** of your decision when there is not much difference between the alternatives.
- **Analyse major decisions into 'pros' and 'cons'.** Write down two lists facing each other on a single sheet of paper to see where the decision lies.
- **Make sure you have the right information** and enough of it to make a balanced judgement
- **Ask yourself what is the worst that can happen if anything goes wrong.** If you have been purposeful and business-like in

your assessment, it will rarely prove as disastrous as you fear, and may cause fewer problems than leaving the matter unresolved.

- **Be decisive.** Select a time to implement your decision, and take action. But remember, too much haste spells rashness; too much delay spells indecision.
- **Once you have made your decision, move on to something else** and don't keep going back over it unless new information comes to light.
- **Believe in your decisions, and they will work.**

'If I had to sum up in one word the qualities that make a good manager, I'd say it all comes down to decisiveness. You can use the fanciest computers in the world and you can gather all the charts and numbers, but in the end you have to bring all your information together, set up a timetable and act.'

Lee Iacocca, CEO, Chrysler Motors

Improving Your Communication

Whilst it is often taken for granted, communication is an important management function, and the span of communication required in your appointment is likely to be extensive.
In any normal day, you will need to communicate with superiors, colleagues, and subordinates. You may need to communicate with clients or customers, and with agents or suppliers. You will communicate to give information, and to obtain information. You will communicate by speaking, listening, writing, and reading. You will communicate by your actions, and by observing what others do. It is, therefore, necessary to regard communication for what it is - a valuable skill, and a useful management asset.

Making your communication effective

You know the old saying, 'Engage your brain before you engage your mouth.' It has much to commend it as a communication maxim. Think through the processes involved before you communicate, and you will make your communication more effective.

- **Develop your message.** Be clear about what you want to say, what information you need to provide, and what outcome you are looking for. If necessary, rehearse your verbal message, or re-read your written text to make sure that what you want to communicate is what comes over.

  ☑ I already do this [ ]   I need to revise my approach [ ]

- **Decide how to communicate**. What method of communication should you use? Face to face communication is best for influencing people; written communication is best for getting over detailed information. Some situations require both.

  ☑ I already do this [ ]   I need to revise my approach [ ]

- **Decide how to transmit the information**. Do you need to set up a meeting for face to face discussion? When and where will be appropriate? Should your written message go by letter, fax, or e-mail? Do you need to phone in advance?

 I already do this [ ]   **I need to revise my approach** [ ]

- **Consider its reception**. How will your message be received? Is the timing right? Will everyone who needs to know be able to attend a meeting? Will a posted, faxed, or e-mailed message arrive in time for the recipient to read and digest its content?

 I already do this [ ]   **I need to revise my approach** [ ]

- **State what reaction you want**. You want something to happen, otherwise there is no point in the communication. Make sure you spell it out in a way the receiver is able to understand. You may understand the implications of a detailed technical report or financial analysis, but if the recipient can't, nothing will happen. Tailor your message to the reaction you want.

 I already do this [ ]   **I need to revise my approach** [ ]

- **Use a signal to emphasise your requirement or intention**. If something is confidential or urgent, say so, or mark 'Confidential' or 'Urgent' clearly at the top of written communications, but do not indicate that something is confidential or urgent if it is clearly not. Among other useful signals for written communication are: *'Action required'*, *'No action required; file for reference'*, *'Progress report'*, and *'Information update'*. Be sure to use the correct signal. Misuse of signals may cause recipients to distrust or be cynical about your communications, and you may not get the result you want.

 I already do this [ ]   **I need to revise my approach** [ ]

- **Get feedback**. You will not know if your message had been received and understood and acted upon in the way you want unless your communication includes a feedback requirement. This could be by stating a simple request, 'Please confirm you have received this letter.' or 'Please confirm when you have taken the required action' If there is no feedback forthcoming, don't assume that no news is good news. Where communication is concerned, no news is bad news. If you get no response, check with the recipient to make sure your message has got through.

 I already do this [ ]   I need to revise my approach [ ]

Report writing

Report writing is an essential skill for managers. Well written reports get results. The others get put aside. How you prepare your reports will determine how others will respond to them. The following points will help you develop your report writing skill.

Keep to an effective framework
The following framework is easy for you to use and will help you get your message through to others.

- **State your terms of reference**. These define the authority on which you are acting, and should contain a statement of formal submission. For example, *'I have been asked by the Finance Director to examine and report on the main causes of debt accumulation during the period 1st July 2003 - 31st December 2003. I now submit my report.'* N.B. It is important that you stick to your terms of reference throughout your report. Keep them in front of you as you develop its content.

 I already do this [ ]   I need to revise my approach [ ]

- **Explain the procedure adopted.** Mention the sources from which your evidence/facts are derived and upon which your conclusions are based. For example, *'The conclusions on page 5 were based on information obtained from -*
  1. Interviews with:
     - *Regional Account Administrators*
     - *Divisional Account Controllers*
  2. Analysis of debt accumulation
     - *period July - December 2002*
     - *period July - December 2003*
     - *comparison of 2002 with 2003*
  3. Comparison with DTI industry report July - December 2003.'

☑ **I already do this** [ ] **I need to revise my approach** [ ]

- **Present your findings.** The body of the report will be concerned with your findings, what you have discovered from your sources, the facts. List these findings under appropriate headings. Bear in mind the importance of simplicity. Don't use obscure words or phrases. Be concise. Remove lengthy sections from this part of your report and place them in appendices, but remember to make an appropriate reference. For example, *'Figures in Appendix C show that while debt accumulation was actually reduced in the period July -September 2003, it rose significantly in the following month and remained at a high level through November and December. The reasons for this were ...'*

☑ **I already do this** [ ] **I need to revise my approach** [ ]

- **State your conclusions.** Set out your conclusions clearly, and give each one a separate line or paragraph. For example, *'Based on my findings, my conclusions are as follows:*
     1. ... ...
     2. ... ...'
  In some instances you may need to suggest that further research and/or more detailed information is needed.

I already do this [ ]   I need to revise my approach [ ]

- **Make your recommendations**. Write positive recommendations, and link them to the conclusions of your report. For example, *'Based on the conclusions set out above, my recommendations are as follows:*
  1. That ... ...
  2. That ... ...'

 I already do this [ ]   I need to revise my approach [ ]

- **Compile appendices**. Information such as statistical data, tables, graphs, reports, examples, costings, etc. are better presented at the end of the report in the form of appendices, but remember to refer to them appropriately in the main body of the report.

 I already do this [ ]   I need to revise my approach [ ]

- **Tie it all together**. Particularly in a long report, you will need to include a table of contents, and a brief summary of the main recommendations. This should come at the front of the report. You may want to include an introduction. This should set out the essential background, the objectives of the report, the terms of reference, why the report was requested, and by whom. List all the recipients. This not only provides you with a check that you have covered everyone you want to reach, but will provide a useful list of possible contacts for recipients. Mention any earlier reports if relevant.

 I already do this [ ]   I need to revise my approach [ ]

Presentation

Reports which are not well constructed and not well presented are difficult to read and understand, they make it hard for recipients to gain access to the information they contain, are notorious for being put aside for later reading, then being overtaken by newer priorities, and may finally end up being forgotten. Make sure this doesn't happen with your reports. You will, after all, put a good deal of time and energy into writing them.

The following points will help you get the effect you require.

Written presentation

- **Check spelling, grammar, and 'typos'.** Nothing breaks the attention of a recipient more quickly than spelling errors, poor grammar, and typing misrakes

- **Check appearance.** Is the report visually attractive, well spaced, consistent in its layout, tidy, clean, obviously well prepared, and obviously put together with care? An inexpensive plastic cover, and a title page insert can make a routine document look inviting.

- **Don't just hand it over.** Treat it as the valuable document it is, and 'sell' its significance by briefly quoting its purpose and the important issues it covers or raises.

- **If sending it by post**, include a brief covering letter explaining why it should be read and supported.

- **Be sure to include the costs and benefits** of each recommendation, and draw particular attention to those which reduce costs and increase benefits

- **Consider providing summary sections** on key aspects, if your report is a long or particularly detailed one.

- **Follow up your report** through personal contact after an appropriate interval of time.

Verbal presentation

- **If appropriate, try to get your report on the agenda** of relevant communications meetings and department briefings within the organisation. A formal verbal presentation will help you get your points over. In some organisations, a combination of written report and verbal presentation is standard practice.

- **Always know word for word how you are going to open and close** your presentation.
  - Start by outlining what you are going to say, the purpose of your presentation and why it affects those you are addressing.

- End by stating exactly what you want to happen.
  This will help you create the important strong first and last impressions.
- **Decide whether you are going to use a fully written script or headings**, for example on numbered cards, to act as prompts and reminders. If you use a full script, make it easier for yourself by using short sentences, short paragraphs, short words, and a large, clear, easily read typeface. Leave space between each item.
- **Avoid jargon**, and make sure you explain any technical terms that may be new to your audience.
- **Refer to the report to avoid getting bogged down in details**. For example, *'I've left out the detail on this matter, but if you want to refer to it later, you'll find it on page 3 of Appendix D.'*
- **Try to anticipate questions, arguments, objections**. Think how you should respond to these and make a brief note in your script or prompt card at the appropriate place.
- **Use visual aids** as appropriate. An overhead projector or a flipchart may make it easier to explain detailed items.
- **Rehearse. Rehearse. Rehearse**. Practise how you are going to say things and how you are going to use your visual aids. Poor presentations are usually poor because they have not been sufficiently rehearsed.
- **The best rehearsals are out loud** - try taping yourself and playing back to hear how you sound - but you can also rehearse by going through your presentation in your mind.
- **Inspect the room** before you give your presentation. Make sure that all the facilities you need are available and in working order.
- **Relax** yourself before your presentation begins.
  - Deep breathing helps. Breathe in deeply through your nose. Hold your breath for a normal count of five. Breath out.
  - Positive thinking helps. You know you are the one who compiled the report. You know that it was well researched and well constructed. You know that it contains sound conclusions and realistic proposals. You know that it is important for the business. You therefore know you are the best person to explain why that is and what it means, and that you cannot fail to hold the attention of your audience.

Handling Change

A significant part of a manager's responsibilities is to uphold operational rules and procedures, and ensure that working practices and administrative systems are complied with in order to maintain efficient employee performance. Where any of these are changed, it will be the manager's further responsibility to ensure that the new requirements are put into effect while maintaining, and where possible improving, the previous level of efficiency.

Change is a normal condition of business. It is a continuing process reflecting, on the one hand, external conditions that create fluctuations and developments of the market within which the business operates and, on the other, internal conditions contained within the way the business operates in areas such as organisational form, innovation, the growth of skills and social development. Businesses need to respond to change in order to survive, and managers need to understand the nature of the conditions that are driving change forward in order to put new arrangements effectively into place.

Factors creating external conditions of change may include:

- **Economic**: consumer demand; inflation; changes in interest or exchange rates
- **Competitive**: new competitors; new products; changes in competitors' strategies
- **Technological**: development of new technologies; new materials; improved methods of communication, manufacture, distribution, etc.
- **Legal**: commercial regulations; employment law; product liability
- **Political**: changes in political emphasis, e.g. nationalisation/ privatisation; political unrest or uncertainty
- **Social**: demographic changes; changes in values and beliefs; lifestyle change

Factors creating internal conditions of change may include:

- **Organisational**: structural change; new/changed policies: new/changed procedures; growth; acquisition; divisionalisation
- **Innovative**: new/changed products; new/changed services or techniques
- **Technological**: changes in processes, machinery, skills and knowledge
- **Social**: workplace changes; new/changed employment conditions; changes in employees' values and attitudes

Any of the factors listed may create the need for change, or it may sometimes be the result of a combination of factors, including pressure from both inside and outside sources. Identifying the source, in order to understand the nature and purpose of the change, should be the manager's first step in handling change.

If you are not certain why an item of change is being introduced, make enquiries. Do not guess at the reason or assume its connection with your areas of responsibility. You can only proceed with your part in implementing change if you know for sure what is intended and why. Any uncertainty on your part is likely to be quickly uncovered by those whose activities you need to change. It is therefore essential that before you attempt to introduce change to the processes or procedures or working conditions affecting others, you have fully considered and understood what is involved, and are able to satisfy any questions or concerns that may arise. (See para 2 of *Gaining Commitment*: Module #1)

☑ I already do this [ ]   I need to revise my approach [ ]

Putting change into effect.
As with all other management tasks, putting change into effect needs to be approached in a systematic way. It is likely to involve adjusting how things are done, perhaps even invalidating existing practices and procedures and developing new ones. It may also involve reallocating

duties and, since it is usual for change in one area of activity to lead to changes in others, the revision of interacting arrangements with other departments or clients or suppliers.

Using the following procedure will make it easier to put change into affect.

- Calculate in advance the effects of change on existing arrangements, and prepare any necessary adjustments to practices, procedures, duties, and interactions with others.
- Note potential problems, and have remedies in place before introducing the change.
- Prepare a plan setting out practical steps to introduce the change. Don't try to do too much at one go. Plan to go forward in steps that can be consolidated in sequence. At an early stage, include those directly involved. Discuss arrangements to manage the transition state between the old and the new. Try to reduce resistance by discussing the reasons for change and the expected benefits.
- Make the change, and emphasise the new practices, new procedures, new duties, and new interactions with others to prevent them slipping back to the earlier ways of doing things.

☑ **I already do this [ ]   I need to revise my approach [ ]**

Employee resistance to change

It is frequently a feature of change that, because people become familiar with, and comfortable with, established methods of doing things at work, their initial response to change can be one of resistance. It will be necessary for the manager to overcome any resistance, and in order to do so it will firstly be necessary to make an assessment of the causes.

The reasons for resistance will not necessarily be the same for every employee, but may include the following:

- **Self-interest**: some employees may fear loss of earnings, for example through reductions in overtime, or loss of status or privileges
- **Personal uncertainty**: some employees may worry about the demands of new technologies, for example will they have the skills and knowledge required, or be able to adapt to new ways of working?
- **Mistrust**: some employees may doubt the motives of change, for example will the introduction of new processes or new equipment or machinery lead to job losses?
- **Intolerance**: some employees may fail to see the point in making changes, may want things to remain as they are, and may regard change as an unnecessary inconvenience.
- **Conflict of beliefs and values**: some employees may object to change because it cuts across their strongly held convictions about the way things should be done, for example where there are proposals to change well established working practices, or where a proposal for open plan working requires managers and senior employees to relinquish personal offices.

Overcoming resistance to change

Managers have the authority to enforce change and override objections, and there may be conditions where this is the right course of action to take, but in most circumstances the objective should be to gain employees' acceptance of the intended change and secure their commitment to it by overcoming their objections. How this is done will depend largely on the kind of objection raised, and in some case it may be necessary to use a combination of responses.

There are several different courses of action which can be considered, including:

- **Persuasion**: using logical, and if necessary, emotional arguments to convey the purpose and intention of the proposed change
- **Participation**: involving employees in discussion to identify the need for change and appropriate adjustments to existing methods
- **Facilitation**: helping employees to adjust to the change, for

example by setting a transition period to give them time to adapt. In the case of major change, you may need to arrange transfers or early retirement for employees who cannot adjust.

- **Education**: explaining the need for and consequences of the intended change. If possible, arrange a visit to another department where the change is operating. Provide training in any new skills and knowledge needed.

- **Negotiation**: using bargaining techniques to offset objections with benefits available through new arrangements, for example new techniques leading to better productivity may reduce overtime, but may allow increased piecework earnings, or a productivity bonus, or better rates of pay. (It is important that any arrangements of this kind do not compromise the effectiveness of the change or dilute the overall benefits to the organisation.)

Overcoming resistance to change is not necessarily easy, and can often be a frustrating process.

Even having carefully judged which of these responses, or combination of them, is the best way to overcome resistance, and having achieved some success, there may be some people who will continue to oppose. Where this occurs, you must persevere. Continue to try to show the doubters the benefits of the proposed change, and begin to introduce areas of it where there is a majority of acceptance. Time and the reassurance of seeing others adapt to the changes without encountering disaster and even gaining some benefit from doing so, is likely to help to lessen resistance.

☑ **I already do this [ ]   I need to revise my approach [ ]**

Whatever the circumstances under which you need to introduce change, you will make most progress in securing the commitment of others where they can clearly identify your own conviction of its necessity and your own commitment to the issues, processes, and procedures involved.

Handling Pressure

There is nothing new in being under pressure. It happens to everyone in every job. You will have experienced it already, and will know that being under pressure has to do with the number and nature of the situations you become faced with. Some will be work-related, others will come from outside of work. Some will present you with the opportunity to do things you enjoy; others will present you with the need to do things you do not enjoy. All will have some degree of urgency. There may also be particular conditions attached to some issues which are themselves difficult or worrying, and some may also carry an emotional factor or trigger an emotional response. Faced with these different and sometimes conflicting demands, how you deal with them will make the difference between being able to cope and becoming overburdened.

Responding to pressure

If you are becoming overburdened, a sensible first step is to consider whether you situation is an exceptional one, something that is a one-off or is temporary and will pass (it does sometimes happen like that), or if it is an accumulation of a more permanent nature. In either case there are things you can do to reduce the pressure and regain control.

If your situation is an exceptional one-off or temporary demand, its cause and what needs to be done to deal with it will be evident from what is happening. Do not allow it to remain unattended to. A positive, timely response to correct or remove the cause will quickly put you back in control. Make arrangements to deal with it as soon as you can. Possible courses of action that will give you scope to do this include:

- re-schedule priorities to take action, but keep key results in focus
- adjust planned arrangements to buy time or resources
- assign someone to deal directly with the situation and report back
- delegate more, if necessary on a temporary basis
- get temporary help

☑ **I already do this** [ ]   **I need to revise my approach** [ ]

If your situation is a more permanent one, an accumulation of different pressures where the volume of demand is becoming overwhelming, it is unlikely to be as straightforward to deal with. But there are still sensible, progressive steps you can take.

- **Start by discarding the thought that everything is on top of you.** The 'everything' you are worried about is made up of individual causes.
- **Isolate them.** Write them down if necessary, identify those that you can most quickly and easily deal with, and take action to correct or remove them as soon as possible. This will relieve some of the pressure, and will enable you to get a better view of the more difficult matters and what you might need to do to resolve them.
- **Having reached this point, repeat the process.** Identify those that you can most quickly and easily deal with, take action to correct them or remove them as soon as you can, and step by step you will find yourself regaining control of your situation.

☑ **I already do this** [ ]   **I need to revise my approach** [ ]

Are you the cause?

If the problem persists, or if it is not easy to identity its causes and what needs to be done to deal with them, you may need to consider that the source of your pressures is yourself, that you have a busy and demanding work schedule that it is not being managed as well as it should be. If you suspect this is the case, there are still some easily undertaken actions you can take to improve your situation, to avoid becoming overburdened and to develop a more positive response to potentially difficult situations.

- **Check out your time management system.** Feeling under pressure often stems from feeling you just don't have enough time to do everything, or enough time to do things as carefully and thoroughly as you would like. If you are having to leave some things out, or if some things are having to be left unfinished in order to keep pace with your schedule, or if too many errors are cropping up in things you have done, it does not necessarily mean you have too much to do. It may very well mean that you are not as organised as you could be. Check yourself out. Ask yourself these questions:

- Are you planning and prioritising your activities?
- Are you focusing on key result tasks?
- Are you delegating where you can?
- Are you making the best use of the time available?
- Are you operating a time management system at all?

☑ **I already do this [ ]** **I need to revise my approach [ ]**

- **Review your perspective.** It is worth remembering that there will be pressure of some kind in every job. How you view it is a very personal matter. What is very pressurising for one person may be entirely acceptable for another. For example, do you think - *'I hate this job. There's simply too much to do. I don't even get time to think.'* or *'I love this job. There's loads to do. I never have time to get bored.'*

  If the job is making you feel under more pressure than you can accept, try discussing your situation with others who are in a similar appointment, or have held a similar one, and who appear to be enjoying it more than you do. You may learn things that will help you reduce the pressures and enable you to adjust your perspective.

☑ **I already do this [ ]** **I need to revise my approach [ ]**

- **Review your response to change.** Because it contains elements of the unknown and can generate uncertainties, change can introduce additional pressures. If you are concerned about the effects of an item of change, ask questions. Get as much information as you can. If you don't understand all the implications, you may be worrying needlessly. Keep an open mind. Get things in their proper perspective. Check out key features. Look for benefits, but don't ignore possible drawbacks; discuss them. There may be more benefits than drawbacks, or even all benefits and no drawbacks. Make any necessary adjustments ASAP. The sooner you get them into place, the sooner you will begin to gain control, and the sooner the pressures will be reduced.

 I already do this [ ]   **I need to revise my approach** [ ]

- **Review your relationships with others**. If your relationships are creating unnecessary pressures, try to understand why. Causes can be:
  - the level of demands - yours or theirs
  - conflict of standards, values, or expectations - yours or theirs
  - neglect of needs - yours or theirs
  - dismissal of concerns - yours or theirs
  - invasion of space or authority - yours or theirs
  - absence of appreciation - yours or theirs
  - inadequate communication - yours or theirs.

Try to be proactive. Take the lead. Take control. Value each person as an individual. Discuss any unresolved issue, and adjust your response accordingly by trying to understand the other person's point of view while trying to get them to understand yours.

- Be realistic in your demands, and require others to be realistic in theirs.
- Discuss standards, values, or expectations and encourage acceptance of yours.
- Respond to other peoples' needs and require them to respond to yours.
- Respond to their concerns and require them to respond to yours.
- Acknowledge the space or authority of others and require them to acknowledge yours.
- Acknowledge good effort and ability at every opportunity, and you will gain the appreciation of others.

- Communicate, communicate, communicate, and listen, listen, listen.

 I already do this [ ]   I need to revise my approach [ ]

- **Learn to handle blame and criticism**. You can give them or receive them. Either case can generate additional pressure, but you can reduce the pressure with the following steps.
  - Find out what has gone wrong and why.
  - Take action to recover control of the situation ASAP.
  - Do not pass the blame if the fault is yours, accept it and correct it.
  - If the fault is someone else's, don't just complain, use the situation to show how to deal correctly with it in the future.
  - Check if lines of communication have been crossed and put them right.
  - Respond proactively - learn from the mistake and take remedial action.
  - Once remedial action is in place, move on. Don't dwell on something that won't happen again.

 I already do this [ ]   I need to revise my approach [ ]

Being assertive

Letting yourself be pushed around by what is happening, or by what other people say or do is certain to leave you feeling under pressure. But be careful how you respond. Don't make the mistake of thinking you are being assertive when, in reality, you are being aggressive, hostile, domineering, or are being manipulative, sly or dishonest. Being assertive is none of those. It is about being in control of your situation, and being able to carry your intentions forward in a positive way without anxiety and without denying the rights and concerns of others.

If you behave assertively, you will be assertive. To do that you will need to **look assertive**.

- Maintain steady eye contact. Don't look away. Don't stare
- Keep a relaxed, but serious facial expression. Don't frown. Don't giggle.
- Keep relaxed gestures. Don't point. Don't pound fists. Don't fidget.
- Keep a business-like posture. Don't be threatening. Don't slouch.

You will need to **sound assertive**.
- Keep a moderate voice volume. Don't shout. Don't mumble.
- Keep a moderate speaking rate. Don't be too hurried or too slow.
- Use a firm tone of voice. Don't sound angry, sarcastic, disinterested.
- Be fluent. Don't use fillers - like, okay? you know? know what I mean?

You will need to **use assertive language**.
- Speak in complete sentences.
- Be direct, clear, concise when making statements.
- Avoid unnecessary descriptions - very, extremely, incredibly, huge, etc.
- Avoid unnecessary fillers - sort of, kind of, know what I mean.
- Avoid labelling and name-calling - dull, lazy, stupid, irresponsible, etc.

 I already do this [ ]   I need to revise my approach [ ]

Be assertive when making requests.
- Ask specifically and directly for what you want. Don't hint. Don't demand. Don't manipulate.

 I already do this [ ]   I need to revise my approach [ ]

Be assertive when saying 'No.'
- Say it directly, without lengthy excuses or apologies. Don't be abusive. Don't be hurtful, but don't feel guilty.

☑ **I already do this** [ ]   **I need to revise my approach** [ ]

Be assertive when giving criticism.
- Be direct, clear, honest, constructive. Don't be aggressive. Don't be sarcastic. Don't belittle the person.

☑ **I already do this** [ ]   **I need to revise my approach** [ ]

Be assertive when accepting criticism.
- Listen to the criticism. Think how you can put it right. Do it better next time. Don't pass the buck. Don't be defensive. Don't be resentful. Don't whine, plead, or make excuses.

 I already do this [ ]   **I need to revise my approach** [ ]

Other steps to consider

● **Develop a support network**. When you are under pressure, the support of others can be invaluable. Talking things through can help to:
- clarify the situation
- put things in the right perspective
- sort out the issues - real or imagined
- get it off your chest.

You may hold back from asking for support because you don't want to appear unable to cope, or you fear your request for help might be refused. If that is the case, think through some preparation in advance.
- Consider **how** to ask. Be factual/specific. Say what you want, but remember you are asking for support, not asking someone to solve your problem. e.g. 'I'd value your view of my proposal.' NOT 'This is the situation. What should I do?'
- Consider **when** to ask. Ask as soon as you feel the pressure mount. Don't leave it to go away. But show respect for the other person's time. Ask when it would be convenient to discuss.

- Consider **who** to ask. It has to be someone who will appreciate what you are talking about - a colleague or a senior.
- But if you really have no idea about how to handle the situation, it is only fair to the person whose support you are seeking to let them know.

 I already do this [ ]   **I need to revise my approach** [ ]

- **Start your day right.** Getting off on the right foot is important. The first half hour of any day at work will set the pace for the rest of it. If you begin your day with enough time to check out the up to date position and make any necessary adjustments to tasks or staffing before the day's activities begin, you will be able to anticipate where any problems or pressures are likely to arise. With this foreknowledge you will be better able to control what is happening, and better able to reduce the pressures on yourself. Without it you will be catching up for the rest of the day. You will not properly be able to control what is happening, and will be bringing unnecessary pressures upon yourself.

 I already do this [ ]   **I need to revise my approach** [ ]

- **Review what is happening elsewhere.** You are just as likely to experience pressures from outside of work as from work itself. They can arise from any area of your life; from family matters, other personal relationships or interests, your health, your finances, or even problems experienced travelling to and from work. There is not always an easy solution to any of these situations, but there are steps you can take to reduce the pressures upon yourself.
    - Begin by examining what you can and cannot influence or control. There will be things that you can do nothing to influence or control. For example, there will be nothing you can do to reduce the volume of traffic during each morning's rush hour, but there may be other aspects of that situation that

will be open to your influence and control. Leaving home five or ten minutes earlier, you might find the roads are clear, or perhaps there is a different route that avoids the worst bottlenecks. By concentrating like that on those aspects of each situation that you can influence or control, you may be surprised at how much you can do to improve your situation.

 I already do this [ ]   I need to revise my approach [ ]

- **Nurture your relationships**, both inside and outside of your immediate family. They should be mutually supportive. Conflicts and disagreements with those closest to you can be a substantial source of pressure, and there may be much you can do to alleviate the tensions. Are you being as tolerant as you could be for the views of others, as considerate of their needs and interests? Are they being as tolerant and considerate towards you? Is there a way reaching common ground? Make it your priority to find one.

 I already do this [ ]   I need to revise my approach [ ]

- **Take care of yourself**. Watch your diet, and monitor your intake of alcohol, tobacco, caffeine, and sugar. A well-balanced nutrition programme will help to make you feel good. It will enhance your emotional well-being, and will contribute to maintaining the energy levels you need to deal effectively with demanding situations. Keep yourself fit without becoming obsessed with fitness. Give yourself time to relax and refresh your body and mind. Leave work at work, and take up a leisure activity instead.

 I already do this [ ]   I need to revise my approach [ ]

- Learn to recognise and monitor the symptoms of mounting pressure. Are you becoming irritable, aggressive, tired, unable to sleep well? Are you putting things off, keeping too much to yourself, having too much alcohol or too many cigarettes? These are all signs of mounting pressure. If you identify any of them in your own behaviour, do something about it. Talk to someone, call a friend, take the dog for a walk. Then come back, look for those aspects of the situation you can do something about, and start to get things under control.

☑ **I already do this [ ]   I need to revise my approach [ ]**

Remember - everyone experiences pressures. How much they are allowed to dominate what you do is largely up to you. You may not be able to control all the factors involved, but you can control your response. And you can take action to improve your situation, to avoid becoming overburdened, and to develop a more positive response to potentially difficult situations.

PR: Promoting the Business Image

Public Relations (PR) is an increasingly important aspect of business activity. Its value is reflected in the growing number of businesses who develop a PR department to promote the organisation's image in contacts with the outside world and to handle communications about the nature and intentions of the organisation in ways that will be beneficial to its business interests.

Key responsibility for PR activities may rest with a senior Board member or with an appointed PR Manager, but by the nature of the authority they express on behalf of their company, all managers become its ambassadors. Particularly in business contacts with people outside the organisation, such as customers, clients, suppliers, government and local authority agents, and the general public, what managers say and do will determine much of how the organisation is regarded.

How managers conduct themselves will contribute to their company's image, growth, and survival, and steps that can be taken to improve that contribution include the following.

● **Keep aware of the organisation's public relations objectives**. What is it trying to convey? How is it trying to convey it? Consider the difference between PR at Harrods and a Virgin Megastore. Both are highly successful, but have very different PR objectives and very different PR styles. Your organisation has its own PR objectives and its own PR style, and it is important that you know what it is and reflect it in the things you do.

☑ I already do this [ ]   I need to revise my approach [ ]

● **Accept a share of responsibility for promoting company image and reputation**. Taking a share of responsibility for PR is not just about the things you do yourself, but includes encouraging others to become involved, and being prepared to speak out if you consider someone to be acting in a way that is detrimental to the company's image and reputation. This is not only good business sense on behalf of the organisation, but will promote your own image and your own reputation as a responsible executive and a valuable business person in your own right.

 I already do this [ ]   **I need to revise my approach** [ ]

- **Ensure that all communication conveys a high standard of business professionalism.** Particularly written correspondence with outside bodies and individuals should convey a positive image of business professionalism. Make sure you know how to set out a business letter, and how to start and end it. Remember, letters starting with 'Dear Sir,' or 'Dear Madam,' should end with 'Yours faithfully,'. Letters starting with 'Dear Mr Jones,' or 'Dear Mrs Smith,' should end with 'Yours sincerely.'

 I already do this [ ]   **I need to revise my approach** [ ]

- **Develop good 'customer relations'.** Contacts with customers, suppliers, contractors, and other agencies may be cordial and, where appropriate, helpful, but they should also always be businesslike, and efficient

 I already do this [ ]   **I need to revise my approach** [ ]

- **Keep to specific arrangements.** Arrangements entered into with customers, suppliers, contractors, and other agencies, should always be adhered to. If exceptional circumstances make it impossible to keep to a specific arrangement, the other party must be advised at the earliest date

 I already do this [ ]   **I need to revise my approach** [ ]

● **Make your department PR minded**. Encourage staff members to follow your lead in promoting a positive image of business professionalism in their everyday contacts with people whether inside or outside the organisation. Particularly take the opportunity to get this message over to any new staff being recruited into the department.

☑ **I already do this [ ]   I need to revise my approach [ ]**

Required Personal Enhancement

Whatever else it requires of you, it is certain that your appointment will need you to maintain a programme of personal enhancement in order to keep pace with the functional, organisational and technical changes that occur within your company as a natural consequence of its business progress and its responses to shifts in trading conditions and methods, as well as advances in technologies.

The extent of these changes within a single career span can be very extensive, and in some instances very rapid. Now more than ever, managers are subject to a continuing state of change with which they are expected to keep pace in order to respond in a way that maintains the company's capability.

Additionally, for most people, a career is not just a ready laid out route that only needs to be followed from A to B to ensure success. There are too many circumstances, both inside and outside their place of work, which are beyond personal influence and control, and frequently the best they can do is to maintain an intention to progress, and a readiness to respond to options and opportunities as they arise.

It is important to consider that:

- it is often very difficult to make firm and detailed long-range predictions about future steps and stages
- you can, however, make short-range plans about some specific things you intend to achieve
- these will need to reflect changes that are taking place in your work, but should provide continuity of purpose, an accumulation of relevant knowledge and experience, and should be consistent with progress towards a longer-term goal

Required personal enhancement is therefore about:

- being perceptive, keeping pace with events and understanding what is going on

- dealing with change and being able to respond to new demands in the job
- maintaining a sense of purpose and the ability to respond proactively to events
- keeping open to options and opportunity, but maintaining a sense of direction, and commitment to the key results activities of your job
- keeping a sense of intention in your career interests, and control over inputs to your career
- trying to ensure that decisions about developments and progress in your job fit well with, and preferably enrich, other aspects of your life, especially close relationships with family and others.

Use the checklist on the next page to find out if you are maintaining an effective programme of personal enhancement.

CHECKLIST OF PERSONAL ENHANCEMENT

Tick as appropriate using the following values.

1: I'm OK on this. 2: Could do more on this. 3: Need to do much more on this.

Required condition   **Status**

                                                           1 2 3

● I keep sufficiently aware of what is happening around me. Not just in my own department, but in the business as a whole, about competitors, about the general economic situation, about Government proposals that might have an effect, about changes in legislation. [ ] [ ] [ ]

● I respond to new information. I make sure I understand it, and evaluate if it is in my business interests, my personal interests, the interests of others with whom I have a business or personal involvement. [ ] [ ] [ ]

● I keep sufficiently aware of possible options and opportunities. I try to make use of these for business and personal interests, I use them to find new ways forward and better solutions to problems. I consider my response to be proactive. [ ] [ ] [ ]

● I respond to changes in my job. I welcome them as opportunities to expand my knowledge and experience, I discuss them with others and invite their input. I am prepared to innovate. [ ] [ ] [ ]

● I respond to new demands in my job. I see them as challenges, not as problems, I see them as steps forward, opportunities to reorganise, restructure and delegate more. [ ] [ ] [ ]

● I feel in control of my situation. I am able to cope with the pressures, able to maintain commitment and enthusiasm, making sufficient progress towards personal goals. [ ] [ ] [ ]

● I keep a balance between the responsibilities and demands of work and the needs and interests of my private life. I don't shut one off from the other. I don't give more attention to one than the other. I find ways that enable me to adjust comfortably between them. I find it easy to talk to people at home about work, and vice versa. [ ] [ ] [ ]

Personal Progress Review
Module #4

Start date of Module #4: ____
1st review date:_____ 2nd review date:_____

If you have followed the guidance given in the preceding pages, you should have made valuable progress in developing your management knowledge and skills. To evaluate your progress, you should now complete the following section by marking an assessment on each of the rating scales to show the extent of change evident since the start of this module.

Please remember that this programme is designed to help you develop your management knowledge and skills through self-managed active learning. It is you who will make it work, and you who will benefit. The circumstances of your appointment may not make the same degree of progress possible in every area of activity, and in some you may not, at this stage, have made as much progress as you like. If this is the case, don't mislead yourself by marking above your achievement. Build on what you have done, and try again. You will gain most advantage from your efforts by making your assessment as honestly and realistically as you can.

Managing your time

On a scale of 1 - 10, where 5 represents your estimate of the effectiveness of your previous management of time, indicate to what extent:

• you feel more or less able to focus attention on key results areas, and

• you feel more or less in overall control of activities and events as a result of action you have taken.

Less able to focus   Previously   More able to focus
After 1 month: [1] [2] [3] [4] [5] [6] [7] [8] [9] [10]
After 2 months: [1] [2] [3] [4] [5] [6] [7] [8] [9] [10]

Less in control   Previously   More in control
After 1 month: [1] [2] [3] [4] [5] [6] [7] [8] [9] [10]
After 2 months: [1] [2] [3] [4] [5] [6] [7] [8] [9] [10]

148

On a similar scale, where 5 represents your estimate of how much of your time you were previously able to spend in productive activity, indicate to what extent you consider you have been able to increase that time as a result of action you have taken to eliminate time robbers?

Decrease   Previously   Increase

After 1 month: [1] [2] [3] [4] [5] [6] [7] [8] [9] [10]

After 2 months: [1] [2] [3] [4] [5] [6] [7] [8] [9] [10]

Making your decisions

On a scale of 1 - 10, where 5 represents your estimate of your previous decision making skill, indicate to what extent you consider your skill to have improved or worsened as a result of action you have taken.

Worsened   Previously   Improved

After 1 month: [1] [2] [3] [4] [5] [6] [7] [8] [9] [10]

After 2 months: [1] [2] [3] [4] [5] [6] [7] [8] [9] [10]

Improving your communication

On a scale of 1 - 10, in which 5 represents your estimate of the effectiveness of previous communication, indicate to what extent you consider your general ability to communicate has improved or worsened as a result of action you have taken.

Worsened   Previously   Improved

After 1 month: [1] [2] [3] [4] [5] [6] [7] [8] [9] [10]

After 2 months: [1] [2] [3] [4] [5] [6] [7] [8] [9] [10]

On a similar scale, where 5 represents your estimate of the effectiveness of your previous report writing, indicate to what extent you consider your report writing ability has improved or worsened as a result of action you have taken.

Worsened   Previously   Improved

After 1 month: [1] [2] [3] [4] [5] [6] [7] [8] [9] [10]

After 2 months: [1] [2] [3] [4] [5] [6] [7] [8] [9] [10]

On a similar scale, where 5 represents your estimate of the effectiveness of your previous presentation, indicate to what extent you consider your written and verbal presentation has improved or worsened as a result of action you have taken.

Worsened   Previously   Improved
After 1 month: [1] [2] [3] [4] [5] [6] [7] [8] [9] [10]
After 2 months: [1] [2] [3] [4] [5] [6] [7] [8] [9] [10]

Handling change

On a scale of 1 - 10, where 5 represents your estimate of how effectively you handled change on previous occasions, indicate to what extent you consider your handling of change has improved or worsened as a result of action you have taken, or knowledge you have gained, from this module.

Worsened   Previously   Improved
After 1 month: [1] [2] [3] [4] [5] [6] [7] [8] [9] [10]
After 2 months: [1] [2] [3] [4] [5] [6] [7] [8] [9] [10]

Handling pressure

On a scale of 1 - 10, where 5 represents your estimate of how effectively you handled pressure on previous occasions, indicate to what extent you consider your handling of pressure has improved or worsened as a result of action you have taken, or knowledge you have gained, from this module.

Worsened   Previously   Improved
After 1 month: [1] [2] [3] [4] [5] [6] [7] [8] [9] [10]
After 2 months: [1] [2] [3] [4] [5] [6] [7] [8] [9] [10]

PR: External relationships

On a scale of 1 - 10, where 5 represents your estimate of the previous level of your active support of company PR objectives, indicate to what extent you consider it to have increased or decreased as a result of action you have taken, or knowledge you have gained, from this module.

Decrease   Previously   Increase

After 1 month: [1] [2] [3] [4] [5] [6] [7] [8] [9] [10]

After 2 months: [1] [2] [3] [4] [5] [6] [7] [8] [9] [10]

Required personal enhancement

On a scale of 1 - 10, in which 5 represents you estimate of the level of your previous response to required personal enhancement, indicate to what extent you consider it has increased or decreased as a result of action you have taken.

Decrease   Previously   Increase

After 1 month: [1] [2] [3] [4] [5] [6] [7] [8] [9] [10]

After 2 months: [1] [2] [3] [4] [5] [6] [7] [8] [9] [10]

END OF MODULE #4

Total Review of Your Personal Development Progress

This book and its programme provided techniques to help you become more able to develop your management potential, and provide you with a more comprehensive view of your management role. It aimed to give you more confidence in your conduct of your management duties, and to improve your ability to control, organise, and develop the people and activities within the scope of your managerial responsibilities by expanding the skills, abilities, and knowledge you can bring to your appointment.

Think back to the way you performed as a manager immediately before you read the book and commenced your programme and compare that with the way you feel able to perform now.

Using the now familiar scale of 1 - 10, where 5 represents your estimate of your previous management performance, indicate by how many points more or how many points less you consider the programme has:

	Less	More
● improved your understanding of the management role	[ ]	[ ]
● improved your understanding of people	[ ]	[ ]
● improved your development of people	[ ]	[ ]
● improved your project management	[ ]	[ ]
● improved your self management	[ ]	[ ]
● improved the confidence with which you conduct your managerial duties	[ ]	[ ]

If your scores have improved by an average of 1 or 2 points, congratulations! You have clearly worked hard, done well, and have become a better manager.

If your scores have improved by an average of 3 points or more, extra congratulations! You are well on the way to realising your full managerial potential, and clearly deserve an extra cup of coffee or tea.

(BUT SEE OPPOSITE)

Continuing your personal development programme

Because the requirements of business are continuously evolving, the process of developing your managerial effectiveness will not end with the completion of the final project in this programme, but will continue through the responses you make to the changes that will inevitably continue to arise. They will require you to maintain your commitment to achieving high standards of professional performance, and as with all the development guidance contained in this programme, it is recommended that your future efforts in personal development are undertaken in a structured way that will enable you to obtain maximum benefit from learning by experience within the particular context of your appointment.

The following guidance points will help you maintain a successful ongoing personal development programme.

● Discuss new developments, new changes, new demands on your managerial skill with your boss. Gain the benefit of another perspective on what is actually involved. Talking things through with your boss will make sure you are 'both on the same wavelength', and will make it easier for you to obtain any support you need.

● Go forward one step at a time. Don't try to accomplish too much at one go. You do have procedures on pages in Module 4 that will help you to deal with change. Remember that change in one place may necessitate change elsewhere.

● Keep staff members informed. Share new requirements and new objectives with your department. Where possible involve them in planning.

● Don't worry if something doesn't work first time. Do your best, but don't shoot yourself if something goes wrong - just find the way to put it right, and learn from the experience.

● Dig back into your original programme. Use the guidance given in the four modules to refresh your thinking and stimulate ideas about different approaches you might make. If you come up with a workable variation, write it down and add it to your folder.

● Give yourself a bonus for trying and for improving. Each time you successfully respond to a new demand in your appointment, you can reflect that it forms a worthwhile addition to your managerial competence. Feel good about it, and give yourself an extra coffee break or an extra fifteen minutes for lunch on that day to reinforce your achievement. You can be sure you deserve it.

As you will have realised by now, your first quick read through this encouraging book will have left you with a wealth of new ideas and really practical advice about developing your personal skills and knowledge base. Now you will need to revisit each section in turn and take the advice and practical steps at a more leisurely pace, to complete the four-stage programme.

The other books in the 'in Ninety Minutes' series also offer a great deal of realistic, practical and worthwhile advice about a wide range of management and business topics. Take advantage of your introduction through this book to read and use more of these excellent books.

Index

Achievement, 30
Affiliation, 31
Appreciation, 32
Assertiveness, 136
Assessment, 48
Autonomy, 31

Blame, 136
Brainstorming, 94
Business Image, 142

Calculating end results, 98
Care, 37
Celebration, 36
Change, 15, 127
Coaching, 55
Cohesion, 23
Commitment, 28
Communicating, 15, 27, 120
Conflict management, 38
Consultants, 57
Controls, 70
Criticism, 136
Customer relations, 143

Daily task sheet, 112
Debriefings 35
Decisions, 15, 113
Delegation, 66
Developing people, 14, 47
Development Support Review, 51
Disciplines, 69

Empowerment, 63
Enhancement, 145
Equity, 31
Esteem, 31
Evaluating performance, 98
Expectations, 32

External relationships, 15

Feedback, 68, 122

Goal setting, 59, 61
Growing pains, 23

Handling change, 127

Information, 36, 88
In-house training, 56
Internal relationships, 35
Intervention, 40

Job enlargement, 33
enrichment, 34
rotation, 33

Keeping in touch, 52
Key results, 106
team activities, 25

Leadership, 19
skills, 14
Leading and managing, 19

'Management by walking about', 53
Managing a project, 87
time, 105
Mediator, 40
Meetings, 110
Mentor, 10
Mission statement, 21
Modules explained, 12
Morale, 30
Motivation, 30

New staff, 52
Nominal group technique, 94

Objectives, 69
Operational plan, 82
Over-commitment, 110
Overview of the Active Learning, 6

Paperwork, 109
Performance, 53
  standards, 59
Personal development programme, 153
  enhancement, 145
Personal Progress Review, 42, 74, 101, 148
Planning, 80
  a project, 79
  and organising, 14
Power, 31
PR, 15, 142
Pressure, 15, 132
Prioritisation, 108
Problem solving, 14, 36
Problems, 88
Procrastination, 111
Programmed problems, 92
Project, 79
  calendar, 84
  criteria, 14
  management, 78
  report, 99
Public relations, 142
  seminars, 56

Quality circles, 60
Quality control, 59

Relationships, 140
Report writing, 122
Resistance to change, 129

Role re-alignment, 16

Safety and security, 31
Self-actualisation, 31
Self-esteem, 27
Self-managed learning, 55
Self-management, 15
Self-rated assessment, 49
Skills assessment, 47
SMART, 62
Solutions, 93
Strategic planning, 81
Success, 36
Support network, 138

Taking care, 140
Task selection, 107
Team building, 21
Team members' abilities, 26
  purpose and identity, 21
Telephone, 109
Time management, 105
  robbers, 109
Total review, 152
Training, 47
Travel, 110
Two-way commitment, 60

Uninvited visitors, 109

Verbal presentation, 125

Well-being, 36
Written presentation, 125